William P. Walsh

Heroes of the Mission Field

William P. Walsh

Heroes of the Mission Field

ISBN/EAN: 9783337193706

Printed in Europe, USA, Canada, Australia, Japan

Cover: Foto ©Lupo / pixelio.de

More available books at **www.hansebooks.com**

HEROES

OF THE

MISSION FIELD.

BY THE RIGHT REV.

W. PAKENHAM WALSH, D.D.,

BISHOP OF OSSORY,

Author of "The Moabite Stone," etc.

London:

HODDER AND STOUGHTON,

27, PATERNOSTER ROW.

—

MDCCCLXXIX.

PREFACE.

My object in writing the following papers (which were prepared by request, for the members of the Church Homiletical Society, and published in the *Clergyman's Magazine*), was to exhibit not only for the benefit of clergymen, but of laymen also, a broad and connected view of missionary effort from the earliest ages of the Christian Church down to the close of the last century. A very prevalent idea seems to exist that after the first two or three centuries had passed by, there was a total or nearly total cessation of missionary work until a period very little removed from our own time. The sketches here presented will help to remove such a false impression, and to show that in all ages there have been some efforts made for the extension of the gospel, varying indeed in value with the amount of light and spirituality possessed by those who made them, but contributing, even in the darkest days, to the welfare of the world and the salvation of men.

My plan has been to select prominent and typical characters, around whom the missionary efforts of their own or after ages seemed to revolve, and by whom such efforts were either initiated or sustained.

If it be not pretentious to say so, my aim has been to exhibit the progress of the Christian Church from a missionary stand-point, and to show how the various nations and peoples of Christendom received their knowledge of the Christian faith. By grouping the circumstances connected with its diffusion around central characters, one was enabled to do more justice to those individuals who have been selected from the illustrious roll of Missionary Heroes, and at the same time to throw something of the interest which attaches to individual life over the wider ranges of ecclesiastical history.

The writer makes no pretence to originality of thought or to freshness of historic discovery. The facts which he has gathered into so small a compass are culled from the pages of ancient and modern writers; and he can only claim the credit of having brought them together in a connected, and he trusts, instructive, form. The works of Eusebius, Bede, Neander, Merivale, Macclear, and many others who have written the lives of individual missionaries, or sketched the progress of the Church at large, have been ransacked, and their information appropriated; and if I have not in every instance quoted my authority, or acknowleged my obligations, it was only because the character of my work did not render it necessary, and the space at my command did not render it possible. Most of the sketches were written amidst the pressure of new and onerous duties, and I am only too conscious that they necessarily bear upon them the marks of haste and imperfection.

To some who may read these pages, the very names of some of my Missionary Heroes will be strange. If so, I rejoice in giving a wider fame to men who deserve to be better known. Other names, however, will be missed which seem equally deserving of high memorial; but it must be remembered that this is not a history of all Missionary Heroes, but a selection of the most typical amongst them, and of those, moreover, who were sundered far from each other not only by time, but by distinctive peculiarities of work, and position, and character. It will be seen, moreover, that one or two names have been introduced which some might think had better have been omitted, but in my judgment they were necessary to the completion of my plan.

I have not ventured into the records of the present century, because in them the names of Missionary Heroes are so abundant and so distinguished that it would be impossible to make suitable selections, and it would be better to relegate all mention of them to a separate volume. Besides, my design was attained when I had once linked the story of apostolic missions to those of our own times, and the history of the latter is so much better known than that of preceding ages that it did not stand in the same need of an interpreter.

If a perusal of these pages serve not only to diffuse missionary information, but to excite a missionary spirit, and to enlist or increase the sympathies of a larger number in the cause of Christian Missions, my highest ambition in the matter shall have been attained; and if one and another be led through the example of those "Heroes of the Mission Field" to devote their own lives to the same glorious enterprise, my most fervent prayers concerning this humble effort shall have been answered.

THE PALACE, KILKENNY.
December 1878.

CONTENTS.

	PAGE
I. APOSTOLIC AND EARLY MISSIONS: THE FIRST THREE CENTURIES	1
II. ST. MARTIN OF TOURS, A.D. 374-397; ULPHILAS, APOSTLE OF THE GOTHS, A.D. 341-388	25
III. ST. PATRICK (A.D. 432-493) AND HIS FOLLOWERS	45
IV. ST. AUGUSTINE IN ENGLAND, A.D. 596-605; ST. BONIFACE IN GERMANY, A.D. 716-755	67
V. ANSCHAR, THE APOSTLE OF THE NORTH, A.D. 826-865	87
VI. ADALBERT, MISSIONARY AND MARTYR AMONGST THE SCLAVONIANS, A.D. 983-997	107
VII. OTTO, THE APOSTLE OF POMERANIA, A.D. 1124-1139	125
VIII. RAYMUND LULL, PHILOSOPHER, MISSIONARY, MARTYR, A.D. 1291-1315	145
IX. FRANCIS XAVIER, MISSIONARY TO THE INDIES AND JAPAN, A.D. 1541-1552	163
X. ELIOT, THE APOSTLE OF THE RED INDIANS, A.D. 1646-1690	187
XI. HANS EGEDE, THE APOSTLE OF GREENLAND, A.D. 1721-1758	209
XII. CHRISTIAN FREDERIC SCHWARTZ, A.D. 1750-1798	229

I.

APOSTOLIC AND EARLY MISSIONS: THE FIRST THREE CENTURIES.

A MAP of the world, when looked upon with reference to the planting and spread of Christianity, is suggestive of far-reaching thoughts. It presents to the mind most varied and important questions; not only arraying before us the great missionary enterprises of our own day, but carrying us back in thought to ages long gone by, as well as onward to future scenes which, according to the unfailing word of prophecy, are sure to come. Here and there, as we review the past, we call up the history of mighty men who went forth amid the world's darkness to carry the torch of truth into its dark places—some of them men of clearer, and some of them men of lesser light—some of them holding forth the Word of Life in all its divine simplicity—some of them doing their work with erring though earnest hands, unconscious to themselves how much they dimmed the very light which they meant to spread; but still, each and all of them contributing in their time and place to "prepare the way of the Lord."

It is our purpose in this series of papers to sketch the lives and labours of some of these missionary heroes, selecting those who were typical characters, and endeavouring to trace in their work and history the various influences for good or for evil which from time to time have been at work in the extension of the Church of Christ. We shall endeavour, as far as possible, to follow a chronological order, so that the series of lives may fairly represent the continuous history of missionary enterprise from the earliest ages down to the present time. It will not be possible, in such an attempt, to do more than present a general outline of the great subject; but it may lead some of our readers to enter into the investigation of it more fully for themselves; whilst to those who have not time for deeper study, it may supply such general information as may be available for their own satisfaction, and also aid them in bringing before others the missionary subject.

The Acts of the Apostles may be looked upon as the first missionary record of the Christian Church, and although it is mainly taken up with the labours of one man—the great apostle of the Gentiles, who stands pre-eminent even amongst apostolic missionaries—yet it shows us how widely the gospel of Christ had spread even in the apostolic age. Into all the countries bordering upon the Mediterranean the heralds of the cross had carried the glad tidings of redemption. We read of Christians in Rome even before St. Paul visited the imperial city. We read of his intention to visit Spain, and we know how, through his labours, the Church was planted in the great cities of Greece and Asia Minor.

We have no very definite or reliable information with regard to the labours of the other apostles. Various Churches in Europe, Asia, and Africa, some with more, some with less show of reason, claim one or another of "the twelve" as their founders. For example, from a statement in an epistle of Clemens Romanus, St. Paul has been claimed as the apostle of Britain; St. Thomas has been claimed as the founder of the Church in India; St. Bartholomew is said by Eusebius to have preached in Arabia; St. Matthew is reported to have carried the gospel to Ethiopia; and the Church of Alexandria has some show of authority for tracing her history to the labours of St. Mark.

But whatever may have been the special fields of labour occupied by these great ambassadors of the cross, there can be no doubt that, in obedience to its Master's divine command, the early Church went forth to "preach the gospel to every creature." And we must remember that it was not merely by apostolic heralds, and by those duly ordained by them, that the gospel was thus spread abroad. In the life and enthusiasm of their first love, Christians of all ranks and countries spread abroad in their own neighbourhoods the knowledge of the blessed truth which had come home with power to their own souls. In this view of the case every Christian was a missionary. He could not be otherwise; for the separation in life and worship from the surrounding paganism which the adoption of Christianity necessarily involved, rendered them manifest at once to all around them; whilst their own intense convictions and fervent zeal made them thoroughly ready and willing to unfold, to all who inquired of them, the great facts and doctrines upon which their whole conduct was based.

It was this, far more than any special organization in the Church, (though we can see evidences of this latter very early and very clearly,) which led to that wide diffusion of Christianity in the first centuries after Christ, which is so fully admitted by pagan, as well as claimed by Christian authors. And as we look upon the history of the Church in later times, and even in our own day, we cannot but confess how much missionary labour has been crippled and retarded by the absence of that evangelizing spirit which distinguished the early followers of Christ; nay, how much it has been hindered and subverted by the inconsistent and unholy conduct of His professed disciples. What a power in the world British Christianity might be, if those who represent it in all parts of the earth were only true in life and conduct to the name they bear!

The early apologists for Christianity were able to appeal to the altered and holy lives of its professors as undeniable evidences of its truth and power. Heathens, as they looked upon the mutual regard of these early disciples, were forced to exclaim, "See how these Christians love one another!" and, better still, in times of plague, and war, and peril, these very heathens experienced such kindness and assistance at the hands of Christians, as gave the strongest practical recommendation to the new and wondrous faith.

In accounting for the progress of Christianity in that early age, we cannot leave out of sight the miraculous aids which were vouchsafed to it. The power of miracles—notably that of healing, and, above all, the pentecostal gift of tongues—gave an influence, and supplied an instrumentality for the spread of the gospel, the strength and value of which can scarcely be estimated by us; and it is probable that these powers, communicated, as we know they were, by the apostles to their immediate successors, survived, at least in many instances, to a much later period than is commonly supposed.

Even those things which seemed to hinder, " tended rather in those early days to ' the furtherance' of the gospel." The refusal of the early Christians to join in acts of idolatry and superstition soon stirred up against them the injustice and intolerance of their neighbours, and eventually brought down upon them the fierce and continued hostility of the Roman government. During those ten long and terrible persecutions, which were intended to crush them out of existence, not only did their faith increase, but their numbers multiplied. Their constancy and self-sacrifice not only wrung pity and admiration from their enemies, but helped to plant in many a heart, hitherto opposed, a faith and love for the great truths which they adorned and maintained. Their growing numbers invited persecution; but still, persecution only caused them to increase.

Pliny, in his famous epistle, written within fourscore years of the death of Christ, declares that he found the temples of the gods almost deserted; the sacrifices and solemnities neglected, and the sellers of victims complaining that there were no purchasers. He informs us that the number of Christians in his own province (Bithynia) was very great; that "the contagion of the superstition," as he terms it, had reached even to the villages and hamlets; that persons of all ages and both sexes, yea, even Roman citizens, had embraced it; and that unless something was done to check it, the national religion would soon be at an end. And so the whole machinery of the empire was put in force to abolish the new creed. But all in vain; the Church came out victorious from the ordeal. The Emperor Galerius, himself the author of the most terrible of these persecutions, was forced to confess that the power of conviction was not to be overcome by fire and sword, and he issued an edict that "for the future no Christian should be punished or disturbed on account of his religion; since it had been made evident, by the experience of so long a period, that they could in no way be persuaded to desist from their own wilful determination."

This decree of Galerius was subsequently confirmed by Maximian, and at length the conversion of Constantine completely changed the aspect of affairs as regarded Christianity and its relations to the empire, and raised it from being a proscribed and hated creed into a place of imperial honour and magnificence. It is more than doubtful whether this change, welcome and merciful though it was to the troubled and persecuted Church, ministered to a purer and better condition of spiritual life. That it told in many respects disadvantageously upon missionary effort is palpable on the page of history. It left room for insincerity and hypocrisy in many who embraced the faith, and it became the occasion, as we shall see in the course of these papers, for the use of means and motives in the spreading that faith which were altogether unworthy both of it and of its professors.

But at present we are concerned with the three centuries which preceded this time of marked deterioration, and shall glance first at the progress which the gospel had made in that period, and then at a few instances which will exemplify the nature of its progress.

Justin Martyr, who flourished in the

second century, says, "There exists not a people, whether Greek, or barbarian, or any other race of men, by whatsoever appellation or manners they may be distinguished, however ignorant of arts or agriculture, whether they dwell under tents, or wander about in covered waggons, among whom prayers are not offered up in the name of a crucified Jesus to the Father of all things."

Gibbon treats this as a "splendid exaggeration," but still he is forced to admit that a twentieth part of the subjects of the Roman Empire "had enlisted themselves under the banner of the cross before the important conversion of Constantine"; and he adds that the picture which represents the Christian Church as only recruited at that time from the lowest and most ignorant, is drawn by "the pencil of an enemy," and is contradicted by facts. We are not concerned to question Gibbon's calculation as to numbers. If the great and manifold hindrances to the spread of the gospel in that age be duly considered, it is surely no small evidence of success that a twentieth part of the whole Roman Empire should have been won to Christ in so brief a time. But it would be easy to show that his estimate is far too low. Some have even gone so far as to fix it at one-fifth of the entire community, and it is probable that in some districts the Christians were in an absolute majority. Tertullian, who wrote his apology at the close of the second or the beginning of the third century, gives a bold challenge to the pro-consul of Asia, and assures him that if he persists in his cruel intentions, " he must decimate Carthage, and that he will find among the guilty many persons of his own rank, senators and matrons of noblest extraction, and the friends or relations of his most intimate friends." Maximian, in one of the edicts already alluded to, speaking of his own district, says that " almost all " had abandoned the worship of their ancestors for the new faith.

It was the wisdom of the early missionaries to seize on the chief centres of population. "There is the strongest reason to believe that before the reign of Diocletian and Constantine, the faith of Christ had been preached in all the great cities of the empire" (Gibbon, cxv.) Tacitus tells us of the vast multitude (*ingens multitudo*) to be found at Rome even in the days of Nero; and as there was a constant stream of travel, both for war and commerce, between the imperial city and more distant regions, we can well understand how surely and how rapidly Christianity would spread from that place alone. In like manner we gather from various sources how Christian schools grew up at Alexandria, and it is easy to imagine how, from that seat of learning and civilization, the gospel would spread through Egypt and Arabia, and over northern Africa, so that we meet with a council of sixty-six bishops at Carthage so early as A.D. 262; and similar influences were at work in other cities.

So far with regard to the progress and

extent of missionary enterprise. Now let us turn to a few exemplars. Partly from the absence of full and authentic records belonging to that age, and partly because missionary enterprise was then the normal work of the many, and not the peculiar inheritance of the few, there are not many names standing out with special distinctness on the missionary roll. Yet we meet in the New Testament with allusions to Andronicus, Crescens, Aristarchus, Trophimus, Silvanus, and Marcus, as famous amongst a large and devoted brotherhood; and coming farther down the stream of time, we read of the missionary labours of Irenæus and Pothinus in Gaul, and of Pantænus in India. Of the Gallic missionaries we shall speak in our next chapter; of Pantænus we give here the few particulars that are preserved.

He seems, according to Eusebius, to have been sent forth by Demetrius, Bishop of Alexandria, about A.D. 188, in consequence of a request made to him for a missionary by the Indians. It is somewhat doubtful who these people were, for the Greek and Latin writers speak of various nations—Parthians, Medes, Persians, Arabians, and Ethiopians—under that title. Jerome represents Pantænus as sent to instruct the Brahmins, but it is more probable that the Ethiopians or Arabians, who lay near to Egypt, and were therefore likely to apply to Demetrius for a teacher, were the Indians intended. They seem, moreover, to have had some knowledge of Christianity, and to have had the Gospel of St. Matthew among them. Pantænus seems to have been a man of great culture and ability, and to have combined the unusual offices of philosopher and missionary. He was a convert from the doctrines of the Stoics, and it was a remarkable thing to hear such a man delivering public lectures on Christianity in the schools of Alexandria. He won into the ranks of his pupils such men as Clement, who was afterwards distinguished by the name of "The Alexandrian." Clement's conversion had taken place early in life; but having travelled over various countries in search of wisdom, he placed himself with entire satisfaction under the instruction of Pantænus, and succeeded him as a teacher. From him also he probably imbibed that missionary spirit which exhibits itself in his celebrated "Exhortation to the Heathen," and the pupil celebrates his master as superior to all his contemporaries. It was such a man, famous besides, as Jerome tells us, for his commentaries upon the Scripture, and for his oral teaching to the Church, that went forth at this early period to proclaim Christ to the heathen, and it proves that the early Church was willing to give her best and ablest sons to this interesting work.

Exile and banishment were the common lot of Christians in these early days, but they only led to the propagation of the faith. Of this we have a remarkable illustration in the case of Cyprian. He was banished to Curubis, a place about fifty miles from Carthage, and a deacon named Pontius, who afterwards wrote his life, was allowed to accompany him. There, for more than a twelvemonth, he preached the gospel to the large congregations which were attracted to his place of exile, and thus made known the name of Christ to multitudes who till then were ignorant of it.

In a similar way Dionysius, Bishop of Alexandria, when banished by Æmilianus, the prefect of Egypt, because he would not do homage to the gods, found missionary employment at Kephro, a remote district of Libya, to which the gospel had not yet penetrated. He himself gives us the following account of it: "Also in Kephro itself the Lord opened the door to the Word. The first seed of the gospel was scattered by us there; and as if God had led us on that account to them in our banishment after we had fulfilled this call, He brought us away from that place."

Nor was it Christian bishops and Christian clergy only who thus made known the word of truth amongst the heathen. Christians of all ranks took part in this glorious work. Diocletian's persecution drove many of them out of Egypt, Libya, and Syria, and they took refuge amongst the barbarian tribes, and evangelized them. Those who were condemned to work in the mines throughout the empire (and this was a common sentence) carried the blessed message of salvation with them, and again and again we read of their labours and success. As it happened in the persecution that arose about Stephen, "they that were scattered abroad went everywhere preaching the word."

War and the captivities that followed led to like results. In a remarkable book, "De Vocatione Gentium," written in the early part of the fifth century, referring to scenes and times under our consideration, we meet the following striking passage: "The very weapons by which the world is upturned serve to promote the ends of Christian grace. Many sons of the Church, who had been taken captive by the enemy, made their masters the servants of the gospel of Christ, and were teachers of the faith to those whose slaves, by the fortunes of war, they had become. But other barbarians, who aided the Romans in war, learned among our people what they could not have learned at their own homes, and returned to their native land, carrying with them the instruction they had received in Christianity." (Neander, iii. 147.)

The conversion of the Iberians, a race bordering on the Caucasus, presents a notable illustration of this missionary agency, and brings to light a humble but successful labourer. Rufinus heard the story of the cross from the lips of an Iberian chieftain, and Moses of Chorene preserves the name of Nunia as that of the Christian female who was the honoured instrument in the work. She had been carried off as a captive, and had been made a slave. Her devotional life attracted attention and won respect from those around her; and so it happened that when, after the custom of the tribe, a sick child had been conveyed from house to house, in the hope that some one might prescribe a cure, it was brought at length to the Christian woman, who said she knew of no remedy; but that Christ, her God, could help, even where human help was unavailing. She prayed for the child, and it recovered. The queen fell sick; the fame of the cure reached her ears, and she sent for the Christian slave. Not wishing to be considered a worker of miracles, Nunia declined the call. The queen was conveyed to her; the captive prayed, and the queen recovered. On hearing the circumstances, the king was about to send a present, but his wife informed him that the Christian woman despised all earthly goods, and that what she looked forward to as her reward was that the people would join her in worshipping the true God. It made little impression on him at the time, but afterwards, in an hour of peril, he recalled the story, and addressed a vow to the God of the Christians, to the effect that if He delivered him he would devote himself to His service. That vow he kept, placing himself under Nunia's teaching; afterwards, in conjunction with his queen, instructing his own subjects;

and finally obtaining teachers for the full establishment of Christianity in his land.

There was yet another way in which war lent its helping hand to early missionary effort. From a very early period, as we can gather both from the Gospels and the Acts of the Apostles, there were devout men in the Roman army. Some there were, even in those early times, who came to view military life as inconsistent with their Christian duty, but that this was not general is plain from the story of the Thundering Legion, under the Emperor Marcus Aurelius. The story runs, that when the army was hemmed in by the barbarians, and in most imminent danger, this legion, composed of Christians, knelt down in prayer, and obtained deliverance for the imperial forces from the perils that surrounded them. Whether the story be true or false, its circulation amongst the Christians of that age shows that their presence in the army, and that, too, in considerable numbers, was an undeniable fact. And with the Roman eagles flying over the world, and Christian soldiers following them, it is easy to understand how an effective missionary work would be accomplished through their instrumentality. It is calculated than in Britain alone there were no fewer than 64,000 soldiers in A.D. 65; and this alone would account for the early spread of Christianity in these islands.

The Christian soldiers of the empire were just the men to confess their faith and to make it known to others. Indeed, ecclesiastical history informs us that as it was in the army Christians were more especially liable to be noted by their enemies, so it was in the army the first attempts were made upon their fidelity and constancy; and innumerable were the examples given by those heroic men that they were not to be corrupted from the faith of Christ. The story of the Theban Legion, A.D. 286, must have some foundation in fact. Twice, it is said, they were decimated by Maximian, because they would not march against their fellow-Christians in Gaul. But even this cruelty could not shake the firmness of the survivors. In the name of his comrades, Maurice, their leader, declared to the Emperor, that, whilst ready to obey him in all things consistent with duty, they would rather die than violate their duty to God. The Emperor ordered his troops to close round the devoted band, whereupon the Christians laid down their arms and submitted peacefully to martyrdom. This is but a single instance, and there are details connected with it which are probably fabulous, but the reign of Diocletian furnishes copious and authentic records of military martyrs and confessors, and the records prove that these men had the mind and the mettle which would necessarily make them missionaries wherever their lot was cast. Soldiers who refused to wear a wreath of laurel at idolatrous ceremonies, and braved persecution and death rather than desert their principles, were just the men to propagate their convictions, and thus to swell that illustrious band of nameless but immortal missionaries who adorned the first ages of Christianity.

II.

ST. MARTIN OF TOURS,
A.D. 374—397;

ULPHILAS, APOSTLE OF THE GOTHS,
A.D. 341—388.

WE have seen how widely and rapidly the Christian religion had spread throughout the Roman Empire before the days of Constantine. We now turn to the age that immediately succeeded, aud select a few examples of the missionary spirit and labours by which it was distinguished. It was to be expected that the conversion of the emperor, and the consequent establishment of Christianity, would give a fresh impetus to missionary labour, and there is little doubt that they had this effect, especially at first, though it is to be feared that they introduced elements of a more worldly kind, which, by degrees, told unfavourably upon the spread of gospel truth. Long indeed before the days of Constantine, deteriorating influences had sprung up within the Church. Asceticism on the one side, and a philosophising spirit on the other, had begun to overlay the simplicity and spirituality which marked the earlier heralds of the cross; and to these was added, under the new *régime*, a growing love of worldly honour, and a reliance upon human power; still, in despite of these hindrances, and sometimes even in conjunction with them, a way was made for the wider diffusion of " the story of peace." Let us take two memorable instances, one from the history of the Franks, and the other from the history of the Goths.

Gaul had very early received the knowledge of the gospel, but whether from apostolic lips, or from the labours of their immediate successors, it is impossible to determine. Some make St. Paul, and others his fellow-labourer Crescens, to be the founder of the Gallic Church; but it seems certain that before Pothinus and his companions planted themselves in the country, towards the middle of the second century, the gospel had been preached in France. How firmly it took root there, may be gathered from the memorable martyrdoms which took place at Lyons and Vienna in the reign of Marcus Aurelius, and the noble confessions which the Gallic Christians then made in spite of torture and of death. Pothinus, their missionary bishop, laid down his life for Christ, at the age of ninety, and was succeeded in his bishopric, if not in his matyrdom, by Irenæus, the famous pupil of the illustrious Polycarp.

But whilst Christian churches had thus been founded in Gaul, the great mass of the population remained heathen until Martin, Bishop of Tours, appeared on the scene as a missionary, about A.D. 374. His life, written by Sulpicius Severus, bears upon it that love of the marvellous which disfigures so many records of these early times; but sufficient remains, after all allowances, to show that he was a remarkable man, who combined in himself the character of soldier, hermit, saint, and bishop, and in his own rough way contributed in no small degree to the spread of Christianity throughout a vast region.

St. Martin was born in Panonia, and brought up at Pavia. Early in life he embraced Christianity, notwithstanding the violent opposition of his parents; and then betook himself to a military life. This he afterwards renounced in order that he might give himself up entirely to the service of God. He placed himself under the tuition of Hilary of Poitiers, and was soon distinguished by his opposition to the Arians, from whom he suffered much persecution.

Having lived for some time as a monk, in the island of Gallinaria, he contracted that admiration for the ascetic spirit, which, as we have said, had already grown out of mistaken views about the Christian life. It was he who introduced monasticism into Gaul, and established the first religious houses at Poitiers and Tours. At first, indeed, industrial occupations were linked to monastic institutions, and in some instances the disturbed character of the age and countries where Christian missionaries laboured obliged them to live together, for self-defence, in secluded communities; but the underlying evil soon developed itself. St. Martin regarded manual work as a hindrance to devotion, and would allow nothing of the kind amongst his followers, except indeed the transcription of books by the younger brethren. But he found full occupation for their time and energies in combating the idolatry and superstition which reigned around them. Had he confined himself and his followers to the simple preaching of the gospel, and the powers of divine persuasion, it had been well; but carnal weapons of warfare began to be used, if not against the pagans themselves, at least against their idolatries and superstitions. At the head of what may be described as an army of monks, he marched throughout his extensive diocese, destroying the idols, the temples, and the consecrated groves of the heathens, thus instilling into the minds of the population a fear, rather than a love, of the God of the Christians, who enabled them to inflict such fearful outrages upon all which the pagans had hitherto held sacred. We must, however, do this warlike missionary the credit of saying, that whilst he demolished the idols of paganism he proclaimed to their deluded worshippers the knowledge of the living and true God, and the way of salvation through the blood of Jesus Christ. Nor was he altogether unsuccessful. Christianity, at least in its outward form, was widely diffused amongst the Franks, and many were led to a spiritual apprehension of its claims. When he died, two thousand disciples followed him to the grave; the men of Tours and Poitiers contended as to which of them should have the honour of his sepulture; and the rumours and reports of miracles wrought afterwards at his shrine prove at least the estimation in which he was held.

But he was, amongst the missionaries, what Elijah would have been amongst the apostles of the Lamb; and had he lived in their day he would doubtless have brought down upon him, but in severer terms, the rebuke of the Master—" Ye know not what manner of spirit ye are of." He himself was probably free from the spirit of persecution and worldliness which afterwards developed itself, but there can be little doubt that his conduct engendered it in others who came after him. His biographer tells with admiration, that when he was at the court of Maximus he allowed the empress to wait upon him, and that when the emperor passed the cup to him, expecting to receive it back from the bishop, Martin passed it to his own chaplain, as being higher in honour than any earthly king. The story may not be true, but the narration of it shows how this spirit was growing up amongst the ecclesiastics of the time; and certainly the whole bearing and conduct of this martial missionary was calculated to foster it in his followers and admirers.

What St. Martin did through a burning, but mistaken, zeal for truth, was soon attempted from less laudable motives by Christian princes, and led to violent reactions on the part of the exasperated heathen, and in some instances to severe reprisals against those who bore the Christian name. Iconoclasm became a fury; and, despite the eloquent remonstrances of Chrysostom and others, the pathway of Christianity was lighted by the conflagrations of heathen temples and the wild excesses of the injuring and the injured.

St. Martin died in the year 397 A.D., aged 81. Within a century after his death Christianity had become the royal religion of the Salian Franks. King Clovis (mainly through the instrumentality of his wife, Clotilda) became a Christian. Arianism was at this time triumphant, and Clovis seems to have been impressed with the idea (one to which the previous history of Christianity in Gaul might naturally lead him) that he should propagate his orthodoxy by the sword. "And for the first time," says Dean Milman, "the diffusion of belief in the nature of the Godhead became the avowed pretext for the invasion of a neighbouring territory." Forthwith there was a religious war to determine the claims of the rival creeds. Burgundy ran red with blood, and the plains of Vouglé witnessed the utter defeat of the Arians. But the spirit and principles thus unhappily developed in France led to the degeneracy of the Church and the decadence of missionary effort. The masses of the heathen within her pale, and the barbarian races on her borders, remained unevangelized, and so it came to pass that the further spread of the gospel both in France and amongst the Germanic tribes was reserved, as we shall see hereafter, for missionaries belonging to our more favoured isles.

We now turn to a different race, and to the labours amongst them of a very different man. The Goths had already begun to make their presence felt by their incursions into the southern parts of the Roman empire. Some of them inhabited Mæsia and Thrace, and from thence invaded Cappadocia and the neighbouring provinces. In some of these wild forays they had carried off some Christian priests into captivity; and these, by their labours and devotedness, won many of their conquerors from their savage nature-worship, and still more savage barbarism, to the religion and obedience of Christ. These in their turn invited other Christian teachers to come and settle amongst them, and so in a short time numerous churches were founded; and when the Council of Nice was held (A.D. 325) they were represented there by a Gothic bishop named Theophilus, who subscribed its decrees.

Ulfilas (born about A.D. 318) was the immediate successor and pupil of Theophilus; and although his name (Vulfila, or Ulfilas, a wolf) would indicate a Teutonic origin, he is said to have been descended from the Cappadocian captives. To this man belongs the high distinction of being called, and deservedly so, "the Apostle of the Goths." He won the love and confidence of the people by rendering them important services on several occasions in their negotiations with the Roman emperors; and for these services he was well fitted by his relationship with both nations.

It was while he was upon one of these missions to Constantinople that Constantine caused him to be consecrated bishop, by his own chaplain, Eusebius of Nicomedia. On his return to the Goths he applied himself most devotedly to missionary work. The emperor having assigned to his flock a district of country south of the Danube, he crossed that river, and settled there amongst his people. The Goths were at this time in a barbarous state as regarded learning. If they had previously possessed an alphabet, they had lost it in the course of their migrations, and only retained the knowledge of the Runic characters. These, however, were only symbolical, and were, moreover, so identified with their idolatry that Ulfilas set about inventing an alphabet. His letters, five-and-twenty in number, and all capitals, were for the most part derived from the Greek and Latin alphabets; but some he had to invent, in order to express sounds which were altogether unknown in the languages of Greece or Rome.

His next and most important step was to give the Goths a translation of the Bible in their own tongue, and it is here that his chief glory as a missionary lies. He was one of the first, if not the very first, to set the example of giving the barbarians the Word of God in their own language. In speaking of this part of his work Professor Max Müller has well said, "Ulphilas must have been a man of extraordinary power to conceive for the first time the idea of translating the Bible into the vulgar language of his people. At this time there existed in Europe but two languages which a Christian bishop would have thought himself justified in employing—Greek and Latin. All other tongues were considered barbarous. It required a prophetic sight, and a faith in the destinies of those half-savage tribes, and a conviction also of the effeteness of the Roman and Byzantine empires, before a bishop could have brought himself to translate the Bible into the vulgar dialect of his barbarous countrymen."

In this respect he presents a striking contrast to St. Martin of Tours, who relied more upon power than upon persuasion; and it is remarkable that the work thus initiated by the Gothic missionary was more permanent than that of his Gallic cotemporary. It is said, however, that he kept back the four books of Kings from the Goths, under an apprehension that the stories of war and battle therein contained would be too congenial to their ferocious natures, and stir them up to similar deeds of daring. He laid, however, a good and broad foundation for his work; and whilst the great bulk of the Gothic nation were involved in fierce conflicts with the Romans, and were spreading themselves gradually over Gaul and Spain, Ulfilas continued his quiet labours, and ministered to his countrymen upon the slopes of Mount Hæmus.

A considerable part of the Gospels, with fragments from other portions of the version made by this early missionary, are still extant, and throw considerable light upon the ancient language of northern Europe.

His example with respect to Bible translations was soon followed in other lands. One instance may be mentioned. Gregory, "the Illuminator," as he has been designated, introduced the Gospel into Armenia, and made a convert of the king, Tiridates III. Armenia thus became the first country which adopted Christianity as the national religion. But a nobler work was done in the fifth century for that country, when Miesrob, who had been royal secretary, gave an alphabet and a Bible in their own tongue to his countrymen, and thus did for Armenia what Ulfilas had done for the Goths; and Neander informs us that this preserved Christianity amongst the people "even while the country was subjected to such dynasties as were devoted to the Zorastrian or to the Mahommedan religion, and sought to supplant Christianity." It reminds us how by like means in our own day the knowledge and love of Christ were preserved in Madagascar during the enforced absence of the missionaries and the violent persecutions of a relentless queen.

Ulfilas, however, appears to have been much more of a practical than of a theological missionary, and not to have understood or concerned himself much with the intricacies of those deep controversies which at that time agitated the Church of Christ. It is probably in this way we are to account for his not only countenancing Arianism, but, if we are to believe the historians, being the means of introducing it amongst the Goths. He is known to have signed the rather compromising creed of Rimini, but still to have kept up his connection with the orthodox party until the reign of Valens. In the reign of that emperor the Huns had invaded the territory of the Visigoths, and the latter, being in danger of losing their possessions, sent Ulfilas, with other ambassadors, to the court of Valens, to obtain a new settlement. The emperor consented to give up to them certain lands in Mæsia, but with the harsh conditions that they should surrender their arms before crossing the Danube, and give up their children to be educated in different provinces of Asia. It is thought that Valens, who was an Arian, pressed the last-named condition through a desire to introduce Arianism amongst the Goths; and it is said that Ulfilas was persuaded by the emperor and Eudoxius, the dominant Arian bishop at his court, into the belief that the differences between the two parties were unimportant, and that agreement in religious doctrine would render union between them and the Romans more secure.

However this may be, certain it is that after Arianism had been cast out of the Church, and had ceased to exercise the skill and dialectics of the learned, it gained new power and importance by becoming the creed of the vast and barbarous hordes which swooped down upon the decaying empire, and became the source of new life to southern Europe. We have testimony, too, that, notwithstanding their errors, these Gothic Christians displayed in their lives the power of the gospel of Christ. Even Athanasius himself bears witness to the change wrought in them by the power of God. The historian Socrates (iv. 33) recognizes amongst them, although they were Arians, the genuine spirit of martyrdom, and says that "although they erred through their simplicity, yet they despised the earthly life for the sake of the faith of Christ." Chrysostom in after years took a deep interest in the Goths, and had a Church set apart at Constantinople for their worship, in which the Gothic Bible was read, and Gothic sermons preached to them by their own clergymen. In a famous discourse, which he himself preached on one of these occasions, he holds up to the admiration of the refined Byzantines, who looked down upon these Goths as barbarians, the transforming power of Christianity as exemplified in those whom they thus despised: "Thus," he says, "have you witnessed to-day the most savage race of men standing together with the lambs of the Church—one pasture, one fold for all, one table set before all."

The work of Ulfilas had told effectually upon his people; whilst the Bible-loving, Bible-searching spirit engendered by his translation of the Scriptures gave security to his work. We find Jerome (himself a great translator of the Bible), whilst residing at Bethlehem, receiving inquiries from two Goths about several discrepancies which they had observed between the vulgar Latin and the Alexandrian versions of the Psalms; and he commences his reply to them in these remarkable words: "Who would have believed that the barbarian tongue of the Goths would inquire respecting the pure sense of the Hebrew original—and that whilst the Greeks were sleeping, or rather disputing with each other, Germany itself would be investigating the Divine Word?" Do not these words call up before us the picture of Germany at the

Reformation period, and the influence of Luther's Bible in the native tongue?

Ulfilas died at Constantinople in A.D. 388, whilst mediating with Theodosius on behalf of his Arian subjects. To him belongs the credit in that early age of employing literature and civilization as the handmaids of religion, and of giving the Bible to his countrymen in their native tongue.

III.

ST. PATRICK (A.D. 432—465) AND HIS FOLLOWERS.

WE now turn from the continent of Europe to an island which, though it lay far out of the reach of commerce and civilization, was destined to exercise an extraordinary and wide-spread influence upon missionary labour. How, or when, Ireland first received the light of the Gospel cannot be distinctly ascertained. That it did so at a very early period seems placed beyond a doubt by the testimony of Tertullian and Chrysostom. The former, writing about A.D. 200, asserts that "even those parts of the British *isles* which were unapproached by the Romans were yet subject to Christ;" the latter, about A.D. 390, says, "Although thou didst go unto the ocean and those British *isles*. . . . thou shouldest hear all men everywhere discoursing matter out of the Scripture." St. Patrick himself, who on account of his great exertions in spreading the truth has well been called "the Apostle of Ireland," evidently admits, in his celebrated "Confession to the Irish people," that a Christian community existed in the country before he visited it. Still, to him may be attributed the full evangelization of the land, and, as a consequence, the foundation of those Christian seminaries which his followers planted at Iona and Landisfarne, and from which, during several succeeding centuries, a stream of missionaries issued forth to evangelize other lands.

Bishop Wordsworth, in his famous Westminster sermons on the Irish Church, has shown how at the very time that Germany and Northern Europe were sunk in heathenism, Ireland was not only rejoicing in the light of truth, but diffusing it throughout those benighted regions. Nay, more, he proves that it was by her instrumentality a considerable part of England and Scotland were converted to the Christian faith.

"Truth," he says, "requires us to declare that St. Austin from Italy ought not to be called the Apostle of England, much less of Scotland; but that title ought to be given to St. Columba and his followers from the Irish school of Iona." We shall therefore go back to the days and labours of St. Patrick, and then briefly sketch the labours and efforts of some of his successors.

St. Patrick, who was born about A.D. 372, speaks of Benaven in Tabernia as his birthplace; but it is uncertain whether this was Boulogne in France or Kilpatrick in Scotland. His father, Calpurnius, was a deacon, and his grandfather, Potitus, a priest; his own name originally was Succath, but he afterwards, according to a prevalent custom in those days, took a Latin name—that of Patricius. We have the great advantage of possessing a sketch of his life written by himself—the "Confession" already alluded to. It is free from those extravagant statements which abound in the hagiology of after ages, and gives us a very clear idea both of his religious views, missionary spirit, and extensive labours.

At the early age of sixteen he was carried captive into Ireland; and thus the land which was to be the scene of his future ministry became the birthplace of his spiritual life. "There," he says, "the Lord opened my heart to a sense of my unbelief, and taught me to remember my sin, and to be converted to the Lord with all my heart." Six years of painful discipline were passed, as he tended the sheep of his heathen master; but "this," he adds, "was for my good, because by these means I was reformed by the Lord, and He hath fitted me for being at this day, what was once far enough from me, that I should concern myself or take trouble for the salvation of others, when I used not to think even of my own."

Having escaped from his captivity, he seems to have been taken captive a second time; but finally returning to his parents, he resolved to prepare himself for missionary work amongst the people whose spiritual darkness had awakened his deep compassion. It appears, moreover, that he had a remarkable dream which greatly influenced his future course. He thought that he saw in this dream a man bringing him a letter from Ireland, and that he heard a voice saying to him, "We beseech thee, holy youth, come and dwell amongst us." He experienced no little opposition from his parents, who were unwilling to give up their long-lost son, or to permit him to return to the scene of his privations; "But," he says, "by the guidance of God I in nowise consented, nor gave in to them ; yet not I, but the grace of God which prevailed in me, and I resisted them all, in order to come and preach the gospel to the people of Ireland." His motives are simply and beautifully set forth in another passage of his Confession, where he writes, "I declare solemnly in truth, and with rejoicing before God and His holy angels, that I never had any occasion, except the gospel and its promises, for ever returning to that people from whom I had made my escape."

As far as can be ascertained from other sources, he appears to have studied sacred literature under St. Martin of Tours, whose missionary labours were described in our last chapter, and by whom, probably, he was ordained; and then he seems to have studied under Germanus at Auxerre, and also in the monastery of Lerins, in the South of France. Thus equipped for his great work, he returned to Ireland about A.D. 432, and commenced his arduous labours.

There is no evidence that he received his commission from Rome; indeed, all the evidence goes the other way, as has been clearly shown by Dr. Todd in his valuable work on "The Life of St. Patrick." A missionary named Palladius had preceded him to Ireland, A.D. 431, and was sent by Pope Celestine, but he had no success, and at once returned. Prosper, the secretary of Celestine, who records the unsuccessful mission of Palladius, makes no mention whatever of St. Patrick, and it is remarkable that Bede also, who was strongly attached to the Roman see, and would be glad to record anything that redounded to its credit, though he mentions Palladius, omits all reference to St. Patrick. The church which was established in Ireland by this eminent missionary long maintained its independence, and was distinct both in doctrine and discipline from the Latin Church. It is remarkable, too, that in most of those points in which it differed from the Roman, it agreed with the Eastern Church, and that it claimed its descent, through the Church of Gaul, from the Evangelist St. John. We cannot enter further into this interesting question of Irish independence, except to mention, as an illustration, that when the English Church at the synod of Whitby (A.D. 664) adopted the Roman mode of keeping Easter, St. Colman, Bishop of Landisfarne, resigned his bishopric, and retired with his followers to Ireland, rather than adopt the Roman use.

Many of the questions which were raised by the see of Rome in its dealings with other churches at that time were (like this concerning Easter) of comparative unimportance; but they were disastrous in their consequences, when decided in the interests of the Papal chair; for they gave occasion for advancing its claims, and of crushing out those who opposed them. England, after some resistance on the part of the ancient British Church, early succumbed to this foreign influence; but for many centuries after St. Patrick the Church of Ireland maintained its independence, and did not finally lose it until the invasion of Henry II.; when the enactments of the synod of Cashel (1172) reduced it to conformity with the Church in England, which had then become entirely Romanized.

But to return to St. Patrick. His knowledge of the language and customs of the people had fitted him to prosecute his work with the greater readiness; and although he met with great opposition at first, both from the heathen priests and princes, and frequently was in peril of his life, he eventually succeeded in establishing Christianity upon a firm basis throughout the land. To him Ireland owes the Primacy of Armagh and her ancient episcopate. To him, and to his life-long labour of three-and-thirty years, she owes the kindling of that light of the knowledge of Christ throughout the island, which, amidst many rude changes, has never since been extinguished.

One memorable scene from his life deserves a special record. He and his companions had arrived on an Easter Eve at Tarah, the chief seat of monarchy. The king and a vast concourse had assembled to celebrate one of their heathen festivals. It appears to have been connected with the ancient fire-worship; and a law existed that on this particular evening no fire should be lighted until a blaze from the royal hill of Tarah gave the signal. The missionary band, probably not aware of the existence of this law, lighted their evening fire, and the astonished Magi represented to the king that unless this fire was at once extinguished it would overcome all their fires. How little they knew what depth of meaning lay in their angry prediction!

The king was soon face to face with the unprotected missionary, and we may conclude that St. Patrick's conduct was both wise and conciliatory; for, instead of vengeance and expulsion, he received permission to preach the next day before the royal assembly; and that memorable Easter-day, if it did not lead to the conversion of the king, ultimately led to the conversion of some of his family, and to a wide and effectual opening for the spread of the Gospel throughout his dominions. It was upon this occasion that St. Patrick composed the famous hymn which has been called his "Breast-plate." It is such an expression of earnest faith and prayer, and gives besides such an insight into the purity of his views, that we have appended to this paper a poetical translation, by James Clarence Mangan, which has the great merit of being very literal, and at the same time gives a good idea of the beauty of the original.

This great missionary possessed a wonderful power of attracting to him the noble and the young. As an illustration of this we may mention the case of Benignus. St. Patrick had visited the house of a great chieftain, and there preached the Gospel, and won the household to the faith. The young heir of the family was so impressed by the words and manner of the missionary, that he could not be separated from him, notwithstanding all the entreaties of his kindred. He devoted himself to the service of God, accompanied St. Patrick through all the dangers and sufferings of his missionary career, and finally succeeded him in the primacy of the Church. In a similar way he is said to have won the heart of one of the native bards, who thenceforth ceased to celebrate the praises of the idol gods, and employed his talents in composing hymns in honour of the Redeemer. It is worth noting that St. Patrick largely availed himself of sacred song in carrying on his missionary labours. For thirty-three years did this indefatigable missionary toil in his Master's service; and when he was laid to rest on March 17th, A.D. 465, he had deservedly gained for himself the title of "the Apostle of Ireland." Not only had he won vast multitudes to the faith of Christ during his lifetime, but he had taken pains that the truth of the Gospel should be continued amongst them after his death, and that it should be spread from them to neighbouring countries. It was for this end he established those missionary schools and colleges for training young men both in secular and sacred culture, which afterwards became so eminent, that, as Bede informs us, "many of the nobility and middle classes too of the English people left their native isle and retired to Ireland, either for the purpose of studying the Word of God, or else to observe a stricter life." (H. E. iii. 27.) Nor was it from England only that scholars flocked to this distant island, which had won for itself the title of "Insula sanctorum;" there is abundant evidence that from the Continent also scholars flocked to this "University of the West," attracted at once by the fame of its piety and of its learning.

But its chief glory consisted in its missionary character. We have already quoted Bishop Wordsworth's acknowledgments as to the missionary work it performed for England and Scotland. This was accomplished chiefly through the schools of Iona and Landisfarne. The former was founded by Columba, or as he is more commonly called, Columbkille ("the dove of the Churches"). He was born amidst the wilds of Donegal, but was of royal lineage. After much labour and some distractions in his native land he settled in Iona about A.D. 563, and founded there the famous school from which Aidan, Finan, Colman, and other famous men went forth to evangelize the greater part of the Saxon heptarchy. Columba himself laboured on for thirty-four years in his adopted home, and from thence carried the story of the cross to the remotest isles of the Orkneys and the Hebrides. Wherever men could be gathered together, he preached the Gospel to them;

and wherever converts were won to Christ, he left some of his followers to minister to their religious wants. Iona became a kind of spiritual light-house amidst surrounding darkness; it shed its beams of culture and religion far and wide, and in a higher sense than any earthly Pharos, realized its blessed purpose—"to give light and to save life." It was no marvel that Aidan, king of the British Scots, went thither to be crowned, A.D. 547, or that Columba was selected to perform the ceremony. No wonder that Dr. Johnson confessed himself overcome by a new enthusiasm when he visited the ruins of this sacred shrine towards the close of the eighteenth century. Landisfarne, which afterwards became so famous as a missionary centre, was an offshoot from Iona, and owed its foundation to one of the most famous of its pupils—Aidan, "the Apostle of Northumbria." It was from these seats of learning and religion that the light which had been almost quenched by surrounding idolatry was kindled once more, illuminating Picts and Scots and Saxons in those dark and troubled ages which followed the mission of St. Augustine to England.

But the successors of St. Patrick did not confine their missionary labours to the British Isles. They went forth in such numbers to the Continent, that they are compared by contemporary historians to "swarms of bees;" and to this day the records of their successes are to be found in France, Belgium, Germany, Switzerland, and Italy. In these different countries they founded religious houses, which in their turn became new centres of light and evangelization; and it is remarkable that their zeal and independence ultimately provoked the opposition of the Latin Church, and led to the extinction of these establishments. It is said that the last of them that survived was Erfurth, memorable as the place from which, in after-days, Luther came forth to give new life to the Christianity of Europe. It was a usual custom with these ancient missionaries to select twelve companions for their work (doubtless not only for mutual help and society, but with a special reference to the number of the twelve apostles), and then to employ them to build up the churches which it was their privilege to have planted amongst the heathen. It was thus that Columbanus went forth with twelve companions to Burgundy, and afterwards placed one of them, St. Gall, in Switzerland, where to this day a canton is named after him as its illustrious missionary. It is to this same Columbanus that Italy owes the conversion of Lombardy, and it was he who planted the standard of the cross at Pavia, Tarentum, and Bobio amongst the Roman Apennines.

At Wartzburg, to this day, is pointed out in their great cathedral the tomb of Kilian, the apostle of Franconia, who, after preaching the blessed Gospel, laid down his life, like another Baptist, for rebuking the vices of the mighty of the earth. At Salzburg you may see the church founded by Virgilius, the Irish bishop, who with his missionary companions went thither in the eighth century, and became the apostle of Carinthia. Fridolin, known from the extent of his labours as "the Traveller," lies buried in the Abbey of Sekingen, where he ended those noble efforts, by which he won so many of the savage Alemanni to the faith of Christ. Batavia, Friesland, and Westphalia are full of the fame of Willibroard, who received his missionary education in Ireland from the followers of St. Patrick. The libraries of Milan preserve to this day the copies of Holy Scripture which belonged to those early evangelists, and which bear witness to their love of Scripture study by the numerous interlineations and comments which they exhibit in the Irish tongue. Even amidst the frost-bound valleys of Iceland relics and records of these labourers have come to light, which prove that neither distance nor difficulty could quench their missionary zeal.

Surely men like these deserve no mean places amongst the heroes of the mission field. The life of any one of them would furnish an interesting theme; but we must be content with this brief and rapid survey of their important and self-denying achievements.

ST. PATRICK'S HYMN.

TRANSLATED BY J. C. MANGAN.

At Tarah to-day, in this awful hour,
   I call on the Holy Trinity!
Glory to Him who reigneth in power,
The God of the elements—Father, and Son,
And Paraclete Spirit—which Three are the One,
   The ever-existing Divinity!

At Tarah to-day I call on the LORD,
On Christ, the Omnipotent Word,
Who came to redeem from Death and Sin
     Our fallen race;
     And I put and I place
The virtue that lieth and liveth in
     His Incarnation lowly,
     His Baptism pure and holy,
His life of toil, and tears, and affliction,
His dolorous Death, His Crucifixion,
His Burial, sacred and sad and lone,
   His Resurrection to life again,
His Glorious Ascension to Heaven's high throne,
     And, lastly, His future dread
    And terrible Coming to judge all men—
     Both the Living and Dead! . . . .

   At Tarah to-day I put and I place
The virtue that dwells in the seraphim's love,

And the virtue and grace
  That are in the obedience
  And unshaken allegiance
Of all the archangels and angels above,
  And in the hope of the Resurrection
  To everlasting reward and election !

And in the prayer of the fathers of old,
And in the truths the prophets foretold,
And in the apostles' manifold preachings,
And in the confessors' faith and teachings,
    And in the purity ever dwelling
    Within the immaculate Virgin's breast, *
    And in the actions bright and excelling
Of all good men, the just and the blest.

At Tarah to-day, in this fatal hour,
I place all Heaven with its power,
  And the Sun with its brightness,
  And the Snow with its whiteness,
And Fire with all the strength it hath,
And Lightning with its rapid wrath,
And the Winds with their swiftness along their path,
  And the Sea with its deepness,
  And the Rocks with their steepness,
And the Earth with its starkness,—
    All these I place,
    By God's almighty help and grace,
Between myself and the Powers of Darkness.

---

* This is unquestionably a mistranslation of the original, viz. :—
  "*In castitate sanctarum Virginum.*"
  "In the purity of Holy Virgins."—*J. H. Todd.*

At Tarah to-day
May God be my stay !
May the strength of God now nerve me !
May the power of God preserve me !
May God the Almighty be near me !
May God the Almighty espy me !
May God the Almighty hear me !
May God give me eloquent speech !
May the arm of God protect me !
May the wisdom of God direct me !
May God give me power to teach and to preach
May the shield of God defend me !

May the host of God attend me,
    And ward me
    And guard me
Against the wiles of demons and devils,
Against the temptations of vices and evils,
Against the bad passions and wrathful will
   Of the reckless mind and the wicked heart,
Against every man who designs me ill,
   Whether leagued with others, or plotting apart.

In this hour of hours
I place all those powers
Between myself and every foe
Who threatens my body and soul
   With danger or dole,
To protect me against the evils which flow
   From lying soothsayers' incantations,
From the gloomy laws of the Gentile nations,
From heresy's hateful innovations,
   From idolatry's rites and invocations,

THE MISSION FIELD.

    Be those my defenders,
      My guards against every ban—
And spell of smiths and Druids and women;
    In fine against every knowledge that renders
The light Heaven sends us dim in
    The spirit and soul of man!

      May CHRIST, I pray,
      Protect me to-day
    Against poison and fire,
Against drowning and wounding—
That so, in His grace abounding,
    I may earn the preacher's hire!

      CHRIST, as a light,
    Illumine and guide me!
CHRIST, as a shield, o'ershadow and cover me!
CHRIST be under me! CHRIST be over me!
      CHRIST be beside me
      On left hand and right!
CHRIST be before me, behind me, about me!
CHRIST this day be within and without me!

    CHRIST, the lowly and meek,
    CHRIST, the All-Powerful, be
In the heart of each to whom I speak,
In the mouth of each who speaks to me!
      In all who draw near me,
      Or see me or hear me!

At Tarah to-day, in this awful hour,
    I call on the Holy Trinity!
Glory to Him who reigneth in power,

The God of the elements—Father, and Son,
And Paraclete Spirit—which Three are the ONE,
　The ever-existing Divinity.

SALVATION DWELLS WITH THE LORD,
WITH CHRIST THE OMNIPOTENT WORD,
FROM GENERATION TO GENERATION—
GRANT US, O LORD, THY GRACE AND SALVATION.

IV.

ST. AUGUSTINE IN ENGLAND,
A.D. 596—605

ST. BONIFACE IN GERMANY,
A.D. 716—755.

HAVING seen how the wave of missionary effort rolling southward from Iona and Landisfarne spread over a great portion of the Saxon Heptarchy, and flowed onward to the Continent, we have now to notice another missionary movement, which, taking its rise in Rome thirty years later than that of Columba in Iona, met and crossed this earlier effort both in England and abroad. This movement naturally links itself to the names of Augustine in England and Boniface in Germany, and some notice of the one is necessary in order to introduce the other.

It is well known that Gregory the Great,

before his elevation to the see of Rome, had himself resolved to become a missionary, and England was the field selected for his labours. The sight of three Yorkshire boys, with their fair complexions and flaxen hair, exposed for sale in the slave-market at Rome, excited the curiosity and touched the sympathy of the Benedictine monk. Learning that they were Angles, or English, he uttered those memorable words, in which pity, piety, and a playful fancy were combined: "Non Angli, sed angeli forent si essent Christiani." He went direct from the market-place to the Bishop of Rome, opened to him the wishes of his heart, and obtained his sanction for the missionary work to which he had so promptly devoted himself.

So much was Gregory beloved in Rome, that the greatest opposition was made to his departure, and he had to escape from his convent secretly, with a small band of his companions. He had already travelled for three days on the great northern road that leads out of the Flaminian Gate, when messengers on jaded horses, bathed in sweat, overtook him with the news that the mob had attacked the Pope in St. Peter's, demanding the instant recall of the missionary, and that they had come by authority of the Pope to require his instant return.

Years rolled by, and Gregory had become Bishop of Rome, but he had never forgotten the Angles, and patiently waited his opportunity. At length it came. Ethelbert, King of Kent, who was also lord of all the kings south of the Humber, had married Bertha, a Christian Frankish princess, who, in the little Church of St. Martin, outside Canterbury, maintained for herself and her companions the worship of the Christian's God. Gregory, determining not to lose such an advantage, sought out Augustine, the prior of his old convent of St. Andrew, on the Cœlian Hill, and despatched him with forty companions to the shores of England, A.D. 596.

We cannot give Augustine an exalted place amongst missionary heroes. Discouraged by the reports which he heard on the way concerning the savage Saxons, he went back to Rome, and sought release from his arduous enterprise. But he had to deal with a nobler spirit than his own; Gregory would hear of no excuses, and sent him forth once more to the work which had been assigned him. We need not here recount minutely the well-known story of his mission;—how Ethelbert with characteristic candour and caution received the messengers of the new faith, and eventually embraced it; how upon Whitsun-Day, June 2nd, A.D. 597, he was baptized in the presence of his wife and his people; how upon the next Christmas Day upwards of ten thousand of his subjects were baptized in the waters of the Swale; how Canterbury, Rochester, and London became the seats of important bishoprics, and the first of these the throne of the English primacy.

There can be no doubt that in some respects Augustine's mission was a success, as in others it was a failure; and it certainly exercised for many centuries a most important influence both for good and for evil upon the character of English Christianity. His compromises with heathenism paved the way for many superstitions; and in the next generation his work stood in need of revival. His arrogance alienated the Old British Church, which was unwilling to bow its neck to the foreign jurisdiction, now for the first time beginning to put forward its unfounded claims. So long as their distinct spheres of labour did not bring them into collision, the conflict between the two parties was not vital: but when their successes touched and over-lapped each other—the one travelling southward and the other northward—it became a crucial question whether Celtic or Latin Christianity was to be supreme in England. "The British and Irish missionaries," writes Neander, "certainly surpassed Boniface in freedom of spirit and purity of Christian knowledge; but Rome, by its superior organization, triumphed in the end, and though it introduced new and unscriptural elements into the Church, it helped, at the same time, to consolidate its outward framework against the assaults of Paganism."

This conflict, however, led to a renewal of missionary effort upon the Continent. The Celtic missionaries, finding no further place at home, crossed the seas, and found abundant employment in those distant fields which had been already opened to them by their predecessors. Thither, too, the Roman missionaries from England, with a zeal that seemed contagious, began to flock, and the same energies and the same conflicts that had been witnessed at home soon manifested themselves abroad.

Amidst these efforts and conflicts the name of Boniface stands pre-eminent. He has won for himself the illustrious titles of "the Apostle of Germany" and "the Father of German civilization." His original name was Winfrid; he belonged to a family of distinction, and was born at Kirton, in Devonshire, about the year A.D. 680. He was destined by his parents for a secular profession; but a visit paid by some of the clergy to his father's house, for the purpose (according to a good old English custom) of instructing the family in religious truth, fired the heart of the youth with a desire for the monastic life. His father was at first much opposed to the project; but, influenced partly by a reverse of fortune, and partly by a dangerous illness, he acceded to the boy's solicitations, and placed him under Abbot Wolfard at Exeter, and eventually at Nuteschelle, in Hampshire, where he received his clerical education.

He was early distinguished by his deep acquaintance with the Word of God, and by his skill in preaching. He was possessed moreover of such tact and prudence, and was of so practical a turn of mind, that he was frequently employed by the community to which he belonged in difficult negotiations, and was even favoured with the confidence of his king. It seemed as if honour and distinction awaited the young ecclesiastic in his native land. But loftier aspirations had taken hold of him, and the mantle of the missionary, rather than the mitre of the prelate, became the one object of his desire.

It happened in this way. Willibrord, a Northumbrian, who had been educated in Ireland, had gone with twelve missionary companions to Friesland. His efforts there had been fiercely opposed by a powerful heathen prince named Radbod; but the tales of heroic endurance and patient faith on the part of the devoted band, which from time to time reached the Anglo-Saxon monasteries, stirred many a heart to its profoundest depths, and amongst the rest that of the youthful Boniface. He communicated to his superior his ardent desire to go to the aid of the missionary party in Frisia. The abbot tried to dissuade him from the dangerous enterprise; but in vain. With three of the community whom he had inspired with his own missionary zeal he sailed for Friesland. The time of his arrival, however, was unpropitious. Radbod was engaged in war with Charles Martel; a fierce persecution against the Christians had ensued; and Boniface was reluctantly obliged to return to his cloister.

It was the winter of A.D. 716; and soon after his return the abbot, Winberct, died. The brethern unanimously wished him to take the vacant place; but his missionary ardour revived; he declined the proffered honour, and was soon on his way to Rome to obtain the sanction of the Pope for a repetition of his arduous enterprise. The following spring he was crossing the Alps with a commission from Gregory II. to preach the Gospel in Germany; and when the summer approached, he commenced his labours in Thuringia. The death of Radbod and the victories of Charles Martel had opened a door for the wider preaching of the Gospel in Friesland, and for three years Boniface associated himself with Bishop Willibrord at Utrecht, and gained successes which surpassed their expectations. Christian churches rose on every side; heathen temples were destroyed; a vast multitude became "obedient to the faith."

And now honour and distinction came to tempt him in a new form. Willibrord, advanced in age, was anxious that Boniface should succeed him in the bishopric; but the ardent missionary, feeling himself impelled by an inward call, and strengthened in his resolutions by a remarkable dream, declined the honour, and plunged into the forests of Hesse. Here, amidst dangers and hardships, with wars resounding amongst the bordering Saxon tribes, and with the scantiest of supplies for himself and his companions, he pursued his labours, founded his first religious establishment, baptized two native princes, and, with their protection and his own thorough knowledge of the native tongue, gained his way to the people's hearts, and won multitudes to the faith of Christ.

It was just at this point that the future character of German Christianity was to be determined. Was it to take a free Christian development, such as previous missionaries had designed fot it, or was it to be brought more thoroughly under the influence of Rome? Boniface was summoned to the imperial city, and desired by Gregory to make confession of his faith. So long accustomed to speak in German, that he could not express himself satisfactorily in Latin, he asked leave to present it in writing. The pontiff eventually expressed himself satisfied; and, in consideration of his labours, consecrated him, on St. Andrew's Day, A.D. 723, a regionary bishop. He bound him, however, by an oath, not only to general obedience, but to have no fellowship or connection with those who did not thoroughly hold with the Church of Rome; but, on the contrary, to hinder them in every possible way. This was an obligation which was evidently directed against the Celtic missionaries, who from the outset had shown much independence; and it was destined to bear fruit, not only in such contests as he carried on against Clement and Virgilius, who were his superiors in learning and catholicity of spirit, but also in the final subjection of the German Church to the authority of Rome.

Much, however, as we regret the issue of that conflict, which postponed the religious freedom of Germany for eight hundred years, it is but just to Boniface to say that neither his allegiance to Rome nor his attachment to the Pope prevented him from fearlessly exposing various superstitions and unworthy practices, which seem to have had the sanction of those in power; and it must be also borne in mind that Romish Christianity in that day, though far from pure, had not as yet crystallized into its subsequent corruptions.

Boniface, having become the legate of Rome, was assiduous in carrying out her plans, and successful in establishing her authority. He went to lengths for this purpose, especially in his political relations with Pepin Heristal, which it is impossible to justify; but he displayed little of that arrogance which marred the work of Augustine in England; and when we turn to the fifteen sermons of his which have been preserved, we find that he was very far from recommending a merely superficial form of

Christianity, or countenancing that compliance with heathen customs which led to so much subsequent superstition. It is remarkable, too, that in that wonder-loving and wonder-manufacturing age Boniface had no ambition to be considered a worker of miracles; nor have his own disciples been able to record any other acts of power concerning him than those which belong to the triumphs of the Gospel over the hearts and consciences of men.

As an illustration of his boldness and success, we may notice his conduct at Geismar, in Upper Hesse. There stood there a gigantic and venerable oak, sacred to Thor, the god of thunder. It had been regarded from age to age with superstitious awe and veneration by the people, and beneath its gloomy shade their most solemn rites had for centuries been performed. In vain had Boniface declared against idolatry; the presence of that sacred tree counteracted, in the minds of his hearers, every impression that he made, and even drew back some of his neophytes into heathenism.

He determined to strike a blow at this superstition, and destroy one sensuous impression by another. With axe in hand, and accompanied by his clergy, he advanced, in presence of the multitude, towards the object of their awe and worship. The pagans looked on with mingled feelings of wonder, rage, and terror, expecting every moment that the sacrilegious assailants would be struck dead by the avenging deity, and the controversy between the old faith and the new settled for ever in their favour. But as the stalwart missionary plied his axe, it was apparent that Thor could not protect his own. A crashing was soon heard in the topmost boughs; the helpless idol thundered to the ground, and lay rent and broken by its fall. Their faith in the dreaded deity had fallen with it; and, as on a like occasion long before, a cry resounded from the multitude—" The Lord, He is God." In order to make the impression lasting, Boniface gave directions that the timber should be used in constructing an oratory, wherein that true God might be worshipped.

We cannot follow the labours which, in conjunction with Wunibald and Willibald, he carried on in Thuringia, Hesse, and Franconia; nor have we time to trace the eventful steps which led to his being appointed archbishop of Mentz, and his disciple, Eoban, bishop of Utrecht.

He was now growing old—the threescore years and ten were almost fulfilled. He had planted the Christian Church amongst a hundred thousand Germans. He had founded nurseries of learning and civilization at Fulda and other places in the Teutonic forests. He had consolidated the scattered work of two centuries, and given bishops and provincial synods for the future government of the Church. He had kept up communications with England, and induced lay and clerical helpers to come from his native land to aid him in his work. He had placed devoted labourers in the remotest districts of the vast wilderness, and cheered them by his exhortations and example. And now he asks, and obtains leave, to appoint a successor, or rather a representative, and to retire to his beloved Fulda, that there he might pray for a blessing on his labours, and close his days in peace.

But once again the missionary fire blazed up in the old man's bosom. He must visit Friesland yet again, to revive the work (which, since the death of Willibrord, had been suffered to decay), and to redeem it from remaining paganism. He was now seventy and five years old, and from that missionary journey he felt that he never would return. He gave his last solemn charge to his successor, Bishop Lull; and then directed that in the book-chest, which he invariably took with him on his journeys, there should be placed the famous treatise of St. Ambrose on "The Advantage of Death," and along with it a shroud, in which his body was to be carried back to Fulda. With a retinue of about fifty clergy and laymen he sailed down the Rhine, was joined by Eoban at Utrecht, and then proceeded towards the eastern part of Frisia.

By many the missionaries were received

with joy; multitudes were baptized, and having received further instruction, were directed to meet Boniface upon the eve of Whitsuntide, in order to receive the rite of confirmation. The Whitsun morning dawned—it was the 5th of June, A.D. 755,—and on the banks of the Buda, not far from Dockingen, he went forth to meet his children in the faith. But the clash of arms and the shouts of an angry multitude soon told that the heathen were at hand. Maddened by the success of the missionaries, they had resolved to dedicate this day to slaughter, and to take vengeance on behalf of their gods. Some of the Archbishop's retinue advised resistance, and would have defended him with their lives; but he stepped forward and commanded them to forbear, and to await with patience the crown of martyrdom. "The long-expected day," said he, "has come, and the time of our departure is at hand. Strengthen yourselves in the Lord, and he will redeem your souls. Fear not them that can kill the body; but cast the anchor of your hope on God, who will soon give you an everlasting reward, and admission to His heavenly kingdom."

It is said that he himself, as the pagans rushed upon him, took a volume of the Gospels, and placing it beneath his head for a pillow, calmly awaited the fatal blow which was to number him with those who sleep in the Lord. Eoban and many of his companions that day shared with him that blessed sleep; and for many a year might be seen, in his beloved home at Fulda, the shroud which he had carried with him to the scene of his first baffled labours, and "The Advantage of Death," which had been sprinkled with his victorious martyr-blood.

His spirit, indeed, lived after him in many of his disciples, who, like Gregory of Utrecht and Sturm of Fulda, carried on the peaceful work which he had loved; but sterner and less Christian characters were soon permitted to appear upon the scene, and terribly was the death of Boniface avenged.

It was only after many a bloody baptism, on many a fierce battle-field, at the hands of the resistless Charlemagne, that the ferocious Saxons were subdued. And after thirty years of bitter strife, during which carnal rather than spiritual weapons were freely used, the Saxons were brought, at least nominally, within the pale of Christendom.

V.

ANSCHAR, THE APOSTLE OF THE NORTH.
A.D. 826—865.

ABOUT a century had passed away since Boniface began his missionary labours in Germany. The wild tribes of Goths, Huns, and Saxons, who had risen on the ruins of the old Roman empire, had been brought to a considerable extent under the humanizing influences of the Gospel. The victories of Charlemagne had spread some degree of civilization over Central Europe, and secured a foothold for Christianity amongst the fierce barbarians. But a new tide of invasion had to be encountered when the wild pirates of the North began to pour down, in the ninth century, upon the shores of France, Germany, and England. Issuing from the dark pine-forests and gloomy fiords of Scandinavia, these terrible marauders swept the seas, invaded every coast, and fought their way into the very heart of the empire. The degenerate successors of Charlemagne beheld their fairest and strongest towns pillaged, burnt, and destroyed, and saw the banners of these hardy Norsemen planted in their noblest provinces.

It was at such a time that the gentle Anschar was raised up by God to carry the Gospel into the ice-bound regions of the North, and to introduce its sanctifying and civilizing influences to the hearts and homes of these fierce invaders. In most respects he was the very opposite of Boniface. Equal to him in energy and determination, he far exceeded him in spirituality and love. "In Boniface," says Neander, "there was a resemblance to the Apostle Peter; in Anschar, to the Apostle John. In Boniface there was more of ardent, impetuous power; in Anschar, more of quiet, but active love." The former was more fitted to produce immediate and visible results; the latter to nurse and cherish those faint beginnings which would ultimately ripen into abiding greatness The Lord of the harvest had work for each of them to do, and doubtless chose and fitted His instruments with reference to that work; and certainly in the case of Anschar He gave a signal illustration to the world of the mighty power of love.

We must glance for a moment at the savage worship which distinguished these hardy Scandinavians. It seems probable that the early Teutonic belief recognized a Supreme Being—Odin, or Wotan—the Creator and Ruler of all, without parts or passions, and who could only be worshipped amidst the awful solitudes of the dark forest or consecrated grove. But this belief was soon lost amidst the darkness and materialism of hero-worship and nature-worship. A complicated system of debasing mythology sprang up. Thor, "the Thunderer," and Tyr, "the god of battle," and Freyer, "the god of harvest," amongst countless other deities, demanded homage; and to these were appended a race of cruel fiends and mighty giants, as Loke, "the backbiter of the gods," Fenris, "the Wolf-god," and Hela, "the Death-god," with numerous others, who must be appeased by bloody victims, and even by human sacrifices. In times of great calamity the kings themselves had to lay down their lives, and well-attested instances are given of monarchs killing their own offspring to avert the wrath or win the favour of the dreaded Odin. Such was the creed of these fierce barbarians, as it is preserved to us in their sacred Eddas and Sagas, which tell us, moreover, of their coveted paradise—the great Walhalla, with its bloody wars, its riotous revelry, and sensual indulgences—meet counterpart beyond the grave of those scenes of strife and horrid orgies in which they gloried here on earth.

The first mission to these dark and dauntless pagans was organized in the year A.D. 826. It was a mission to Denmark; and some account of the introduction of the Gospel to that country will be the more interesting, if we bear in mind that a king of Denmark (Frederick IV.) was the first king in modern times who originated and supported missions to the heathen in connection with the Reformed Faith. Harold Klak, king of Jutland, and his queen, had been on a visit to Louis le Débonnaire. It is said that they went for aid in adversity, and received it on condition of embracing Christianity. At all events, they were baptized in the great cathedral of Mayence. The Emperor was anxious to send back with his ally a zealous preacher of the Gospel, who might confirm the royal converts in their faith, and spread the knowledge of Christianity throughout Denmark. But at that time it was no easy matter to secure the services of a missionary. The reports which, from time to time, had reached the continental churches concerning the sanguinary practices of the Norsemen, and the visible proofs which they had on all sides of their appalling ferocity, were enough to deter the boldest heart from venturing amongst them. At length Wala, who was the abbot of Corbie, informed the emperor that he knew a man of such heroic faith and earnest zeal, that he only longed for the opportunity of undertaking such an arduous task, and of laying down his life, if necessary, in the cause of Christ.

This man was Anschar; and we must now go back a little in his history to see how God was preparing him for this great occasion. He was born not far from Corbie, in A.D. 801, and received, as many a noble spirit has done before and since, his first religious impressions from a pious mother. He lost her when he was only five years old; and though for a time, amidst the companionship of rude schoolboys, he forgot her early teaching, yet it came back to him in a remarkable way. He beheld her in a dream, surrounded by bright and happy spirits, and was warned that if he wished to join her in heaven, he must forsake sin, and devote himself to Christ. This made a deep impression on the child, and, young as he was, he resolved to dedicate himself to a religious life. For this purpose, according to the custom of those mediæval times, he went into the neighbouring monastery.

While he was there, then only thirteen years of age, news reached the community that the mighty Charlemagne was dead. It was an event to make even the most thoughtless thoughtful, and Anschar's pious spirit was deeply moved within him. He had seen the emperor in all the pomp of power and blaze of victory, and now the mighty conqueror lay subdued by death. He doubtless heard of the impressive way in which that crowned corpse was buried in the wondrous tomb which he had prepared for himself at Aix-la-Chapelle. "There," says Palgrave, in a well-known passage, "they reverently deposited the embalmed corpse, surrounded by ghastly magnificence, sitting erect on his curule chair, clad in his silken robes, ponderous with broidery, pearls, and orfray; the imperial diadem on his head, his closed eyelids covered, his face swathed in the death-clothes, girt with his baldrick, the ivory horn slung in his scarf, his good sword 'Joyeuse' by his side, the

Gospel-book open on his lap, musk and amber and sweet spices poured around, and his golden shield and golden sceptre pendent before him." All this was intended to impress men with the majesty of Charlemagne, but its effect on Anschar was to show him the vanity of human life, and fill him with more earnest resolves to live for immortality.

His ardent spirit was now visited with other dreams and visions. He saw, as it were, the glories of another world; he experienced the aspirations of a higher life; he felt himself summoned to the special service of his Divine Master; he thought he would be privileged to wear the crown of martyrdom. One of his dreams bears so directly upon the work of grace in his own soul, that it deserves to be recorded. He thought he saw the Saviour in His glory, as John saw Him at Patmos, and he threw himself at His feet "as dead." With loving look and gentle voice he heard his Saviour say, "Confess thy sins, that thou mayest be justified." Anschar answered,

"Lord, why need I to do this? nothing is hidden from Thee." The Lord replied, "I indeed know all things; but it is My will that men should confess their sins to Me, and that they may receive forgiveness." Thereupon Anschar knelt down and poured out his sins and prayers before Christ. "Fear not," were the blessed words that followed; "I am He that blotteth out thy transgressions." The vision vanished; but Anschar awoke in the happy confidence that the Lord Jesus had forgiven his sins for His own name's sake; and in the power of that confidence he lived and laboured for Him all his life long.

But it was not only, nor indeed chiefly, by dreams and visions of the night that the future missionary was prepared for his work. He became a deep and earnest student of the Word of God, and in the retirement of a neighbouring vineyard spent much of his time in prayer and meditation. As he advanced to manhood his talents became manifest, and at the age of twenty-five he was placed in charge of a foundation called

New Corbie, on the banks of the Weser, and here, in labouring and preaching amongst the surrounding poor, he gained much practical experience.

It was at this period of his life, on the recommendation of Wala, that he was sent for by the emperor, and requested to undertake the mission to Denmark. He at once assented, but it was under the deepest sense of his own unworthiness, and in entire reliance upon Divine aid. When his brethren at Corbie heard that he was about to resign all his hopes and prospects, and go forth to preach to the savage heathen of Scandinavia, they used all their arguments and entreaties, and when these failed, their ridicule, also, in order to deter him. But his was a heart of dauntless bravery and steadfast faith. Autbert, the steward of the monastery, a man of noble birth and noble spirit, was struck with admiration. When all hung back, and no one could be found to accompany the missionary, he asked Anschar whether he still kept to his resolution, and received this reply: " When I was asked whether I would go for God's name among the heathen, to publish the Gospel, I could not venture to decline such a call. Yes, with all my powers I wish to go hence, and no man can make me waver in this resolution." "Then," replied Autbert, "I cannot find it in my heart to let you go alone: I will go with you!"

Harold Klak himself was not disposed to give much encouragement to the missionaries; but it so happened that in the voyage to Jutland he sailed in the same ship with Anschar, and before they reached their destination the zealous missionary had won the king's respect, and awakened in his heart an interest in his proceedings. His first work was to found a school in Schleswig, in which he might train Danish youths for the ministry. It is memorable as having been the first Christian institution on these barbarian shores, and Anschar soon filled it with boys received or purchased from the savage population. For two years he and his companion preached throughout Jutland and Cimbria. They had much opposition to encounter, and not being able to obtain a servant, had to perform the most menial offices themselves. Still they went on zealously, and not altogether unsuccessfully, in their work; but at the end of that period disappointment and disaster came: Autbert sickened, returned home, and died; rebellion broke out; Harold was expelled from his kingdom, and Anschar was unwillingly obliged to retire from his first field of labour.

But his zeal was not quenched, and just at this juncture a new sphere was providentially opened to him. The king of Sweden had sent ambassadors to the court of Louis on a political mission in A.D. 829. In the course of their visit they informed the king that some knowledge of Christianity had been brought to their country by means of Christian captives who had been carried thither by Swedish pirates, and that, as a consequence, many of the people were anxious to have Christian teachers. Once more Anschar was summoned to the palace; once more he accepted an arduous duty; and soon, in company with a friend named

Witmar, he set sail for Sweden. They were attacked by pirates, plundered of everything they possessed, amongst other things less valuable, of several volumes of the Holy Scripture which they had collected for the use of the mission. They reached the shore with nothing but their lives; but when Anschar's companions proposed to return, he nobly replied, "What may happen to me is in the hands of God; but I have made up my mind not to return until I discover whether it is God's will that the Gospel shall be published in this land."

Destitute and half dead, they reached Sigunta, the ancient capital, and were graciously received by the king, who gave them permission to preach to his subjects. Already the nucleus of a Christian Church existed amongst the poor captives, who had been so long deprived of the means of grace; and with their aid and the blessing of God the work of evangelization went on. It was not long before Herigar, the king's counsellor, embraced the faith, and threw his influence into the scale.

Returning to the court of Louis with a letter from the Swedish king, Anschar was made archbishop of Hamburgh, which was to be henceforth the centre for the northern missions. It was thought needful in those times to obtain papal sanction for such arrangement, so Anschar visited Rome to receive this sanction, and then returned to Hamburgh. Here he laid himself out to consolidate and extend his work, redeeming from slavery a number of Danish youths, and educating them for the work of the ministry. Meantime the Swedish mission had been entrusted to Bishop Gauzbert, who was at first most favourably received; but the pagans, alarmed at the spread of Christianity, rose in rebellion, and expelled him from the land, murdering his nephew, and devastating the newly-planted church. Meantime sorrows and disasters thickened around Anschar. The Norsemen poured down on Hamburgh, sacked the town, and reduced the church to ashes, so that he had to go forth as a wanderer through his diocese, depending upon strangers for the very food he ate, and saddened most of all by the news of what had befallen his beloved Swedish mission. Yet, amidst all this, he never lost faith in God. It is said that as he gazed upon the desolation wrought at Hamburgh, he calmly exclaimed, " The Lord gave, and the Lord hath taken away; and blessed be the name of the Lord." Words which had been spoken to him from a deathbed, by Archbishop Ebbo, who had been his fellow-helper in the work, came now with comfort to his soul: " Be assured, brother, that what we have striven to accomplish for the glory of Christ, will yet, by God's help, bring forth fruit. For it is my firm belief, nay, I know of a surety, that though the work we have undertaken among these nations is for a time subject to obstacles and difficulties on account of our sins; yet it will not be lost or perish altogether, but will, by God's grace, thrive and prosper, until the name o the Lord is made known to the uttermost ends of the earth."

Such faith and patience were sure to be

rewarded. Horick, the king of Denmark, had taken an active part in the incursions which had destroyed Hamburgh. But Anschar knew the power of prayer and the might of love. He never ceased to pray for those who had caused such desolation; and strange to say, he was chosen by the emperor to go as an ambassador to Horick, and so won the confidence and respect of this fierce king, that he was permitted to revive the mission in Denmark, to erect a church at Schleswig, and to scatter the word of life widely throughout the kingdom. Persecution, indeed, broke out a second time, and the work seemed crushed; but again, through God's mercy, light shone upon the darkness; Anschar was recalled, and the progress of the gospel was more rapid than before.

But Anschar's large heart was not satisfied; he longed to revive the Swedish mission also, and tried to persuade Gauzbert to revisit it. But Gauzbert was afraid; and our missionary hero, having applied to one and another to undertake the work, and finding none that would make the venture, resolved to go himself. What influence he had gained over his old enemy, Horick, may be gathered from the letter which he obtained from that monarch to Olaf, the Swedish king: in it he states that "he had never in his life seen so good a man, or so trustworthy, and that for this reason he had allowed him to do what he wished respecting Christianity in his own land, and hoped King Olaf would do the same, for he certainly aimed at nothing but what was good and right." Such a testimony reminds one of a missionary in later times, when Hyder Ali, in the midst of a vindictive war with the Carnatic, sent orders to his officers—"Permit the venerable Father Schwartz to pass unmolested, and show him respect and kindness, for he is a holy man, and means no harm to my government."

On his arrival in Sweden, Anschar found the pagans in arms against the new religion. His companions pronounced it madness to proceed, and urged him to use the presents (which he had brought for the king) to save his life from the ferocious multitude. He replied, "I will give nothing to redeem my life; and if the Lord so wills it, I am ready to suffer tortures and even death here for His name's sake."

Nothing is more remarkable in the life of Anschar, who, unlike many missionaries of his time, was unsupported by earthly power, than the providential way in which outward circumstances were often made to tell in his favour on the minds of the pagans. Two instances of this occurred upon his second visit to Sweden. Olaf proposed that the question of his admission or expulsion should be determined by the "sacred lots." The assembly met; the lots were cast, and they were favourable. Then an aged chieftain rose and said, "Hear me, O king and people! The God whom we are invited to worship is not unknown to us, nor the aid He can render to those who put their trust in Him. Many of us have proved this by our experience at sea, and in other manifold perplexities. We see our own gods failing us, and unable to help us in time of danger.

Listen then to my counsel, O king and people, and let us not reject what is so plainly for our advantage."

Thus the worship of the true God gradually supplanted that of Odin; and though the conflict between heathenism and Christianity continued long, and was not finally concluded until the reign of Canute, yet in due time the patience and faith of Anschar brought forth abundant fruit. For four-and-thirty years he laboured amongst the fierce Norsemen, seeking in every way their spiritual and temporal good, and winning his way to their hearts by the power of gentleness and truth. Those who at one time had opposed and rejected him, came at last to look upon him as almost divine, and expected miracles at his hands; but he himself disowned such an ambiguous distinction, and said, "One miracle I would ask the Lord to grant me, and that is, by His grace to make me a holy man."

One of his last acts was to check the

slave trade. He sternly reproved the chiefs who were engaged in this nefarious traffic, induced them to set their captives free, and ransomed others from their cruel bondage. He died at last of a painful malady, on February 3rd, A.D. 865. One thought troubled him for a time on his dying bed—" Why had he not been permitted to win the martyr's crown?" It was a vain regret, especially for one whose life had been one long martyrdom; but it soon gave way to the fulness of God's own peace. He spent his last few days in calmly arranging the concerns of his missionary stations; and then, with his eyes fixed on heaven, he entered into rest—these words lingering on his lips,—" Have mercy upon me, O God, according to Thy loving kindness." "God be merciful to me a sinner." "Father, into Thy hands I commend my spirit."

VI.

ADALBERT, MISSIONARY AND MARTYR AMONGST THE SCLAVONIANS.

A.D. 983—997.

Now that we have traced the successes of gospel truth amid the Celtic and Teutonic races, let us turn our attention to its progress amongst the Sclavonic tribes. These tribes, embracing the wild populations that spread over Russia, Poland, Lithuania, and Prussia, were distinguished at first by their quiet pastoral habits; but owing to oppression at the hands of Teutons and Turks, and the bitterness engendered thereby, they became as fierce as any of the other races which had poured down upon the Roman empire.

Their religion appears to have been characterized by a dual system of benignant and malevolent deities, the former being worshipped by gladsome rites of song, dance, and festive offering, whilst the latter were approached with terror and dismay, and were appeased by bloody offerings and even by human sacrifices. In no part of the Sclavonic territories did these dark superstitions take a more awful form than in the regions of Prussia and Livonia. A terrible trinity, known as Percunos, the god of thunder, Potrimpos, the god of harvest, and Picullos, the god of the infernal regions, shared with countless inferior deities the awful homage of the Sclavs. Polygamy existed; slavery in its darkest forms prevailed; even wives were slaves, who on the death of their husbands either ascended the funeral pyre or destroyed themselves in some other way. In this and many other particulars the religious rites of the Sclavonians very closely resembled those of the Hindoos, and it is remarkable that the languages of both peoples have a strong affinity. Infanticide, especially of female children, was common; the sick, the aged, the deformed were put out of the way; and not only were the horses, hounds, and armour burnt along with the corpse of their late master, but many of his slaves, both male and female, shared the same dismal fate.

Such were the Sclavonic tribes, and they were amongst the last in Europe to hear and receive the gospel of peace. It was a dark age when it reached them, and the missionary spirit had almost died out of the Church. The monastic orders, whatever had been their earlier energy and zeal, had sunk down into worldliness and sensuality. The Arabian imposture was making progress. The Saracens had won the Turks to embrace the delusion, and the Turks had rewarded the Saracens by conquering their spiritual teachers, and by laying the foundation of their own empire. The tenth century has been described as "an age barren of all goodness, a leaden age, abounding in all wickedness; a dark age, remarkable above all others for the scarcity of writers and men of learning." It was no marvel that such a period should be deficient in real evangelistic enterprise. "Only when the Church is rich internally," says Neander, "in the gifts of the Spirit, will the Divine life flow over outwardly, and the water of life, while it fructifies the heathen world, will flow back with a blessing to the districts from which it issued : but where the spiritual life is wanting, no salutary influence can go forth on those who are without the pale of the Church. If the salt hath lost his savour, wherewith shall it be salted ? "

It was at a time such as this that Adalbert was raised up to be a solitary but faithful witness for Christ amongst the most unpromising of mankind. A foundation for the Christian Church had indeed been laid in Russia amongst the eastern Sclavs about the time that he carried forth the gospel to the western Sclavs of Prussia; but the movements were distinct, not only as to their origin, but as to their entire character. It may be well to preface the story of Adalbert's work by a brief reference to the origin of a nation and a church which, as Archbishop Trench has observed, "are fresh and young, and only now beginning to play their part in the world's story;" for "with Russia and the fortunes of Russia the future of the Eastern Church is manifestly bound up," and that this " future is a remarkable one it is impossible to doubt."

The Russian kingdom arose under Ruric, a Verangian chief, in A.D. 862. In A.D. 955, Olga, a Russian princess, visited Constantinople, and there embraced Christianity, taking the baptismal name of Helena. She tried to influence her ferocious son Swiatoslav to follow her example, but in vain. He died in battle, and as his son Vladimir seemed more likely to be a docile pupil, missionaries came from all quarters in the hope of making an eminent proselyte. Mahommedans from the Volga, Jews from amongst the Chazars of the Crimea, Christian theologians from Germany, ecclesiastics from Greece, all flocked around the barbaric king. He deferred his decision until he had despatched an embassy to their respective countries, and received its reports. Their accounts were most unfavourable about all the places which they had visited, with the one exception of Constantinople; but concerning the Byzantine capital and its religion, they were lavish in their praise. They described the attractive ceremonies, the thrilling music, the pompous processions, the gorgeous ritual which they had witnessed beneath the dome of St. Sophia, and declared that if God had His dwelling amongst men, it must be there.

The nobles of the court were impressed by the narrative, and said to Vladimir, "If the religion of the Greeks had not been good, your grandmother Olga, who was the wisest of women, would not have embraced it." The king, already impressed by the descriptions he had heard, was still further influenced by this appeal; but what seems eventually to have decided him was, that having sought the hand of Anna, the Emperor's sister, in marriage, he found he could only gain her by accepting Christianity. Under these mingled and by no means exalted motives he was baptized A.D. 988. Forthwith he ordered the huge idol of Peroun to be dragged from its temple, scourged by his horsemen, and cast into the Dneiper. His next step was to issue a royal proclamation commanding all his subjects, on pain of his displeasure, to be baptized. The morrow witnessed a strange scene at Kieff. The inhabitants, rich and poor, with their wives and children, flocked to the river, and standing up to their necks in its waters, whilst the priests read the service from its banks, were baptized in the name of the Trinity, whole companies receiving together the same baptismal name.

Thus it came to pass that, "before the overwhelming catastrophe of the fifteenth century, a nation destined to have an immense share in moulding the future history of the world had received from Constantinople the seeds of the Christian faith, not indeed of that faith in all its primitive purity, for none can give better than what they possess themselves; but what it had, the Greek Church had freely given;"* and there, to use the expressive words of Dean Stanley, "silently and almost

* Archbishop Trench.

unconsciously she bore into the world her mightiest offspring."

One noble work, however, had been already achieved for the Sclavonic tribes, which did something to counteract the evil of these political conversions, and to bring light and peace to many a dark and burdened heart. This was the translation of the Holy Scriptures into the native tongue by two brothers, Cyril and Methodius, the sons of a Greek nobleman of Thessalonica. They had been sent, towards the close of the ninth century, by the Greek emperor, into Moravia, where the people, Sclavonic by race and Christian by profession, were, in reality, heathen. Their first work was to compose a Sclavonic alphabet, and then to translate the four Gospels, the Acts of the Apostles, and the Psalms into the language of the people. It was a work in which they met with considerable opposition, especially from German ecclesiastics, but it triumphed in the end over all opposition, and proved a source of blessing to multitudes. In such veneration was this version held, that for ten centuries it continued to be used in the Greek Church. It was only so late as the sixteenth century that portions of the Bible were translated into modern Russ, after the old Sclavonic tongue had been for centuries like a foreign dialect.

But we turn now from the wholesale and dubious conversions amongst the Sclavonians of Russia, to the more arduous though less dazzling labours of Adalbert amongst their western kindred. He was born in Prague, A.D. 956, and was descended from a respectable family. Having received his education at Magdeburgh, he returned to Bohemia, and was chosen bishop of his native city in the year 983.

The flock over which he was called to preside were intractable, and may be said to have been only half-christianized and half-civilized. They combined the superstitions of their ancient heathenism with the tenets of their Christian faith, and virtually lived a pagan life. Adalbert was not deficient in zeal, but he evidently lacked the patience and moderation which such circumstances required. Thwarted, opposed, and disappointed, he again and again forsook his post, and sought in monastic retirement ease for his vexed and righteous soul. Now we find him visiting the famous anchorite, Nilus, in his distant Italian cell, and then returning to his refractory people at Prague. Again we find him resigning a post in which his want of tact made him almost as much disliked as his German nationality. Once more we find him returning, under a sense of duty, but evidently with reluctance, to Bohemia, only to be expelled again by his rude Sclavonian flock.

This third expulsion proved to be the real commencement of his brief but memorable missionary life. He found a temporary home in Hungary under Prince Geisa, who, induced by the influence of his wife, had consented to receive Christian baptism. Neither the prince nor his wife, however, appear to have displayed much of the Christian character, and Adalbert does not seem to have made much impression on them by his teachings. But his labour was not in vain in the Lord. They had a son named Stephen, upon whom the missionary's exhortations and example left a permanent effect. This youth became afterwards the first king of Hungary, and it was mainly owing to his influence that Christianity was established in that kingdom. Indeed, it is remarkable that neither here nor elsewhere was Adalbert permitted to see much fruit of his own exertions; but he cast his bread upon the waters, and it was found "after many days."

In all probability, it was his want of apparent success in Hungary that led him to Prussia—a region to which no missionaries had as yet directed their steps, and it was, moreover, sunk in the deepest and most appalling heathenism. He sought and obtained from Boleslad I., Duke of Poland, the use of a small ship and a guard of thirty soldiers, and with these soon reached Dantzic, then a border town on the confines of Poland and Prussia.

This was in A.D. 997, the last year of his troubled life. Fortunately no opposition was made to his landing, and he began at once to preach the gospel to the rude barbarians. For the first time in his life he obtained a ready auditory, and not a few listened to the word of life, and embraced his message.

Encouraged by this success, he determined to visit the opposite shore; but being anxious on his arrival to preclude all suspicion from the minds of the heathen, and to cast himself wholly upon the protection of the Lord his God, he sent back the vessel and his guard, retaining with him only a fellow-labourer named Benedict, and a pupil called Gaudentius. On reaching the curious lagoon called the "Frische Haff," or Fresh Sea, he and his companions proceeded in a little boat to an island at the mouth of the river Pregel. Here, however, they were assailed by the barbarous inhabitants, who fell on them with clubs. Adalbert, who, according to an old missionary custom, appears to have been singing at the time, had his psalter knocked out of his hand, and was stunned with a heavy blow from an oar, which felled him senseless to the ground. His first words on recovering were, "I thank Thee, O Lord, that Thou hast counted me worthy of one blow for the sake of my crucified Redeemer."

Leaving this inhospitable shore, they succeeded, with great difficulty, in making their way to Samland, on the opposite side of the Pregel. Here they were met by one of the chiefs, who brought them to his village, and having gathered all the inhabitants together, demanded of the strangers who they were, and what was the object of their visit. Adalbert, in gentle tones, explained who and what he was, and then added, "It is on account of your salvation I have come hither, that you may forsake your gods, which can neither hear, nor speak, nor see. I am come to tell you of the one living and true God, your Creator, for there is no God beside Him; that so, believing in His name, ye may receive eternal life, and be made partakers hereafter of His eternal bliss."

But his hearers were filled with wrath. Gnashing their teeth and flourishing their clubs, they exclaimed, "These are the men who make our crops to fail and our herds to die! Let them depart instantly from our land, or they shall meet death for their delay. They may think themselves fortunate that they have come so far unhurt. We only know of one law and one manner of life, and they who serve another unknown God must leave the land, or be beheaded the next day." Forthwith the missionaries were put into a boat, and compelled to leave the coast. Adalbert was inclined to linger in the country, even at the risk of life. He thought that by adopting the dress of the barbarians, and working at some handicraft, he might in time dispel the prejudices of the savage population. But a different issue was at hand.

Having tarried a few days at the place to which they sailed, Gaudentius in the night-time told his master of a dream which had just been sent to him: "I saw," said he, "in my dream a golden cup upon the altar, and it was half filled with wine. No one was near, and I wished to drink of it; but One drew near, and said that this could not be, for that it was not for me, or any other man, to drink of that cup; and that it was reserved for my bishop, for his spiritual refreshment on another day." Adalbert, who, in common with many good men of former times, made the mistake of courting martyrdom, considered this dream an intimation that he was to wear the martyr's crown, and said to his pupil, "May God bless this vision; but we may not trust a dream which may only deceive." When daylight dawned, they pursued their way through the forests, and as they went made the woods resound with psalms. At noon they halted, and partook together of the Lord's Supper. Having refreshed themselves for the journey, they were about to proceed on their way; but Adalbert felt weary, and having repeated a verse of Scripture and sung a psalm, he composed himself to sleep. His companions, exhausted with their fatigues, soon followed his example. But that sleep had a terrible awakening!

They were startled therefrom by the yells of a band of savages, some of whom bound them as prisoners, whilst others demanded their instant death. Adalbert, with marvellous calmness, addressed his two companions, and said, "My brethren, be not troubled! We know that we suffer this for the name of our dear Lord, whose might is above all might, whose beauty is above all beauty, and whose grace is inexpressible. What can be more blessed than to lay down life for Him?" The words had scarce escaped his lips, when a pagan priest rushed upon him from the infuriated crowd, and with a lance transfixed him through the breast. Others followed, and plunged their spears into his fallen body. Adalbert raised his eyes to heaven, and with a prayer for himself, and another for his murderers, he died, like the first martyr, calling upon God.

Thus perished the first missionary to Prussia, on the 23rd of April, A.D. 997.

His work seemed to be frustrated, and his short life to have been almost spent in vain. But who can doubt that his work was with his God, and that his life, though nearly fruitless in the eyes of men, and seemingly unsuccessful as compared with that of others who had employed more earthly means for spreading the gospel, was not in vain? Other missionaries followed in his steps, and other martyrs laid down their lives amongst the Sclavonic tribes. Well had it been for the fierce Sclavonians had they listened to those gentle teachers, and accepted the message of loving mercy at their hands. With sorrow and shame we turn to the story of their subsequent subjugation; for with regard to many of them, it was rather a work of extermination than of evangelization which we have to record. We look down through the two dark centuries that followed, and see the "Order of Teutonic Knights" and the "Brethren of the Sword" carrying the spirit of a fierce and sanguinary crusade into the heart of Europe, and coercing its remaining heathenism to embrace the religion of the Cross. Alas! for the days when, by the authority of Christian bishops, and in the name of the Christian religion, and of its Divine Founder, such deeds were perpetrated for the propagation of the Faith, and such retaliations provoked as make our ears to tingle, and the very blood to run cold within our veins!

It is in contrast with such means as these, as well as in contradistinction to the spirit and temper of his own dark times, that the name of Adalbert stands out upon the page of history as a faithful missionary; not indeed without faults and failings, for he was a man of like passions with ourselves, but with a heart that burned with love to Christ, and melted with pity for his fellow-men. Even if he had never been enrolled amongst "the noble army of martyrs," he would have deserved a place amongst the heroes of the mission field.

VII.

OTTO, THE APOSTLE OF POMERANIA.

A.D 1124—1139.

MORE than a hundred years had passed away since Adalbert had preached the Gospel and laid down his life as a martyr amongst the Sclavonic tribes of Prussia. Little had been done in the meantime for the real extension of Christ's kingdom. Nestorian missionaries indeed had been propagating their doctrines with considerable success in the wilds of Tartary, and the Greek Church had been putting forth some of its energies towards the East; but in Europe the eleventh century was not favourable to missionary effort. The Church of Christ had become militant; but it was so in the worst and most carnal sense of the word. Fanaticism had succeeded to Christian zeal; and violence and coercion had taken the place of mild persuasion and faithful testimony. Princely authority and priestly power had usurped the place of holy lives, and so it came to pass that whilst the borders of the visible Church were extended, the spiritual kingdom of Christ made little progress.

Towards the close of the century, however, there was a partial revival of religion. The stir of the crusades which awoke Europe from its stagnation seems to have been accompanied by a shaking amongst the "dry bones" of Christendom. As a result of this we meet with a renewal of missionary effort; not marked indeed by its ancient purity and power, but still exhibiting, amidst manifold errors and deficiencies, somewhat of its ancient zeal and self-devotedness. And so the twelfth century presents us with a few names which ought not to be forgotten when we are taking account of the heroes of the mission field. Amongst them we may name the scholarly and pious Vicelin, who toiled amidst so much discouragement amongst the savage

Wends, and his patient pupil, Meinhard of Yxhull, who founded the first Christian Church amongst the fierce Livonians; and more especially the indefatigable Otto, who shines forth amidst the darkness of his age as a self-renouncing and devoted missionary of the cross.

We select the latter as a typical character, not only on account of his personal character and energy, but because his life and labours bring us into contact with the more prominent surroundings of the period in which he lived, and enable us to understand the influences for good and for evil which were at work around him in that almost forgotten time. Moreover, as his efforts were chiefly directed towards the evangelization of the Sclavonic tribes, a sketch of his life will form a suitable sequel to the story of Adalbert, their first and martyr missionary.

The Sclavs who dwelt in Pomerania had hitherto been unimpressed, and indeed we may add unvisited, by the Christian missionary. Their own dark religion and its numerous and well-ordered hierarchy presented serious obstacles to the entrance of the truth. In every town and village their priesthood exercised an all but resistless power, before which even the authority of the secular rulers had often to give way. Their superstitions had culminated into an organized and complex system which seemed impervious to assault. The little they had seen of Christianity was enough to make them hate it with all their heart; for when Boleslav III., Duke of Poland, had subjugated Pomerania, and carried away thousands of its people into captivity, he had, after the manner of those times, forced them, at the point of the sword, to renounce their idols, and to receive Christian baptism.

The first attempt at instructing them in Christianity was made by a zealous but not very prudent Spaniard of the name of Bernard. He presented himself at the Court of Poland, and asked permission to preach to the Pomeranians. Although "the mendicant orders" had not yet sprung into existence, the spirit which gave rise to them had begun to show itself. The luxury and wealth of the existing orders had produced a reaction in the minds of the thoughtful, and it took the form of an extreme but decided protest, when poverty and mendicancy were voluntarily adopted as adjuncts of the Christian life. The Spanish missionary, accordingly, accompanied by his chaplain and interpreter, appeared before the gate of Julin in the garb of a beggar, with bare feet and tattered dress. He doubtless thought that such an illustration of self-denial would make a favourable impression upon the Pomeranians. But he altogether forgot that they were heathens, and that whatever impressions such a garb might make upon men who looked upon self-denial as an element of Christian truth, it was not calculated to produce any favourable results in the case of the heathen, and especially of those who were accustomed to the splendid habiliments of their own exalted hierarchy.

"The people," says Mr. Maclear, "regarded the missionary with profound disdain. When he asserted that he had come as a messenger from God, they asked how it was possible to believe that the great Lord of the world, glorious in power, and rich in all resources, would send as His messenger a man in such despicable garb, without even shoes to his feet." They taunted him moreover with pretending to a divine mission, when in reality (as they asserted) he only wanted to obtain relief for his destitution; and added that if the God he served was anxious for their conversion, He would have sent an ambassador more worthy of Himself and of them.

Bernard, with a zeal that displayed at once his sincerity and his fanaticism, offered to put the reality of his mission to an unauthorized test. He proposed that they should set fire to a ruined house, and that he would leap into the flames: if he came forth from them unscathed, they should acknowledge his authority, and embrace the faith which he proclaimed. The Pomeranians, thinking that the enthusiast was mad, urged him to leave the place; but instead of doing this, he wildly struck down one of their cherished idols. A riot immediately ensued; he was hurried on board a ship, and told that as he was so anxious to preach he might exercise his vocation in speaking to the fishes of the sea and the fowls of the air. So ended the first and abortive mission to the Pomeranians.

It was fortunate that on his return Bernard met with a man who had as much zeal as himself, but far more wisdom and Christian light. This man was Otto, a Suabian of noble family, who had been chaplain to the Duke Wratislav, and now filled an exalted position as Bishop of Bamberg. He heard from the Spanish monk the story of his adventure, and was ultimately led, partly by the monk's solicitations, and partly by those of Boleslav, to undertake the mission himself. Determined, however, to avoid the mistakes of his predecessor, and to adapt his proceedings to the character of the race whom he was about to evangelize, he set out in company with his chaplain Ulric, and seven other clergymen, all supplied not only with suitable raiment for themselves, but with such costly presents for the Pomeranian princes as would make it plain that he did not come in order to obtain anything at their hands.

It was on the 25th April, 1124, that the mission party, with a retinue of waggons, a guard of soldiers, and envoys from the duke, set out upon their journey. Their way led through hitherto untrodden forests and quaking morasses; and it was after considerable risk and difficulty that they found themselves, at the end of six days' tedious marching, upon the confines of Pomerania. Here they were met by an armed band of savages, whose loud voices and flashing knives caused them no little alarm; but it was soon discovered that their chief was friendly, and that his followers were not set on mischief. Passing on towards Pyritz, through a region depopulated by war, the few peasants whom they met on the way were alarmed by the military aspect of the mission party, and flung themselves at the bishop's feet, declaring their willingness to obey his wishes. And here the low standard of missionary work in that dark age becomes apparent; they were baptized upon the spot, with little inquiry and less instruction!

They reached Pyritz in the evening, and as the inhabitants were celebrating a heathen festival, Otto delayed his entrance into the town until morning. The envoys of Boleslav preceded them. And now we come to the curious admixture of the temporal and the spiritual which characterized these mediæval missions. The envoys reminded the inhabitants that one of the conditions of peace between them and their Sovereign was that they should embrace Christianity; and then they informed them that a legate of noble birth was at hand to instruct them —no mendicant like Bernard, but a rich and powerful bishop of their monarch's court, and that they had better not incur the duke's displeasure by declining to receive the teacher whom he had so graciously sent to them.

Otto entered in his episcopal robes, with

his imposing retinue of soldiers and ecclesiastics; and at first the people of Pyritz naturally enough thought that they were deceived, and that an invading army instead of a missionary band had appeared in their midst. Otto, however, soon reassured them. Standing upon an eminence, he thus addressed them: "Ye men of Pyritz, the blessing of the Lord be upon you. We return you many thanks for having refreshed our hearts by your hearty and loving reception. Doubtless you have already heard the object of our coming, but it will not be amiss to remind you again. For the sake of your salvation, your happiness, your joy, we have come a long and weary way. And assuredly ye will be happy and blessed if ye be willing to listen to our words, and to acknowledge the Lord your Creator, and to serve and worship Him only."

Three weeks were spent at Pyritz in preaching to the heathen, and instructing them in the nature of the Christian religion. It is said that seven thousand persons received the rite of baptism, and we cannot but hope that, notwithstanding the strange admixture of methods with which it had been introduced, the Gospel proved to many "the power of God unto salvation." From Pyritz they proceeded to Cammin, where, during forty days of preaching, many others were baptized; and then the mission party turned their faces to the town of Julin, from which Bernard had been so recently and ignominiously expelled. Here they met with the most determined opposition, and barely escaped with their lives. It was evident that earthly pomp and grandeur had as little power to convert the heathen as the most abject poverty and squalor. After much negotiation between the envoys and the populace, it was agreed to abide by the decision of Stettin, which was the wealthiest and most important of the Pomeranian towns.

The people of Stettin, however, received the missionaries with indifference, if not with scorn. "What have we to do with you?" was the universal cry. "We will not put away our national customs, and we are well content with our present religion. Are there not thieves and robbers among you Christians? . . . Keep your own faith for yourselves, and intermeddle not with us." How frequently since that day has the progress of the Gospel been impeded by the inconsistent lives of its professors! But Bishop Otto was a good man. If he could not win the Pomeranians by argument or entreaty, he could at least set before them the charm of a Christian life. He spent several months in Stettin, and exhibited to the astonished heathen such a life of virtue and benevolence as they had never even imagined. He relieved the poor; he visited the sick; he redeemed the captives, and restored them to their friends. His whole conduct was calculated to silence the taunts of enemies, and to win a favourable hearing for the word of life.

During his stay in Stettin, an event occurred which, in the providence of God, made a deep impression upon the people. Two young men, sons of opulent parents, had heard Otto preach, and visited him in private in order to obtain further instruction at his hands. Their visits were often repeated (for Otto had a wondrous power of attracting the young), and at length they declared their wish to receive Christian baptism. Without the knowledge of their parents they were admitted into the Church. The news of their conversion soon spread abroad, and the mother sent word to the bishop that she was coming to claim her sons. Otto, knowing her influence in the city, resolved to receive her in the open air. He was surrounded by his clergy; the young neophytes, still arrayed, according to the custom, in their white baptismal robes, were seated at his feet. A great concourse had gathered to see the strange sight, and to support the mother in making her claim for her apostate sons. As she approached the bishop, the young men rose to meet her, and, overpowered by her feelings, the mother sank prostrate and weeping to the ground. All present supposed that she was overwhelmed with grief at their defection from the ancient faith; but what was their surprise when, on being raised from the earth, and having regained her composure, she exclaimed, "I bless Thee, Lord Jesus Christ, Thou source of all hope and consolation, that I behold my sons consecrated in Thine own sacrament, and enlightened by Thine own truth." Then turning to her sons, and embracing them, she added, "Thou knowest, my Lord Jesus Christ, that I have never ceased for many years to pray for them, and to beseech Thee to do for them what Thou hast done for me."

She then told her history: how, many years before, she had been taken captive, and carried to another land; how there she had heard the Gospel of salvation, and embraced it; how on her return she had been kept back by fear from the open profession of it; and now, by the visit of Otto and the conversion of her sons, she had been led to this avowal of her faith in Christ. Then she blessed God for His mercy in sending the missionaries to Stettin, and addressing Otto, she said, "If you only stay here, you will gain a large church for the Lord; only be not wearied in waiting long, and take my case as an encouragement in your work."

A profound impression was made by this event, and whilst it was at its height a message arrived from Boleslav, saying that he was astonished at the manner in which the people had behaved to the legate; that only for the intercession of Otto he would have punished them severely; but that if they would now listen to his instructions, he would remit a portion of their tribute, and guarantee a lasting peace.

These influences combined in their several degrees to secure an acceptance for the Gospel amongst the men of Stettin; but in order to test their sincerity Otto proposed that they should destroy their idol temples; or, if they feared to do it themselves, that he and his party should be allowed to do it for them. To this latter alternative they consented, and as temple after temple fell, and idol after idol was destroyed, the multitude exclaimed, "What power can these gods possess, who cannot even defend themselves?" Thousands of willing hands were soon aiding in the work of demolition; and before the year had closed a Christian church was erected in the market-place of the city.

Julin followed the example of Stettin; Colberg, Belgrade, and other towns heard the word of life, and multitudes renounced idolatry. Otto, amidst much that was unreal and unsatisfactory, had planted some precious seed, and even reaped a harvest, amongst the most superstitious of the Sclavonic races. He returned to his diocese in 1125, but after a year went back to the scene of his missionary labour. It is no uncommon thing in missionary work to witness a violent reaction on the part of the heathen after much success has been achieved. We have seen this in our own day in Madagascar and New Zealand. It was such a reaction in Pomerania that summoned Otto back; but in this journey he took a different route, and planted the standard of the cross in Wolgast, Gützkow, Usedom, and other important towns. Arrived at length at the scene of his former labours, he had to encounter perils and difficulties innumerable. His life was constantly in danger, but fearlessly and lovingly he devoted himself to his mission, and after earnest and anxious endeavours he beheld a revival of his work, and left it established upon a firmer foundation for the time to come.

We can trace a decided advance in his own Christian life and in his mode of proceeding. He had learned to place more value upon the spiritual power of Christianity than upon its externals, and had seen how dangerous it was to encourage any admixture of paganism and Gospel truth. At Gützkow the people offered him costly presents if he would spare a magnificent idol temple, of which they were very proud. "Would you," replied he, "sow wheat over thorns? I trow not. As you therefore first root out the thistles from your field, and then sow your seed, so must

I take away all that belongs to idolatry from your midst, in order that you may bring forth fruit unto eternal life." The result was that they destroyed the temple with their own hands. He built them a handsome church in its stead; but on the day of its consecration he directed their attention from the outward to the inward, and warned them against placing Christianity in mere externals. He pointed out the necessity for change of heart, and, as a consequence, devotedness of life; then turning to Mislav, the governor, he said, "You, my beloved son, are a true house of God, but you must consecrate yourself to Him entirely; and in order to this, you must release your slaves and debtors." It was "an hard saying," and Mislav felt it to be so; but the persuasions of the missionary prevailed, and the governor at length replied, "Behold, in the name of the Lord Jesus, I give to all their freedom, that according to your word this consecration may be completed in me to-day." The example of this noble deed told powerfully upon his countrymen.

One place, however, resisted all Otto's efforts. This was the Isle of Rugen, which has been well described as "the Mona of the Baltic." It had been for centuries the source and centre of Sclavonic superstitions; it had now become the last stronghold of fanaticism and idolatry. Otto determined, at the hazard of his life, to visit it, and would have carried out his heroic intention if the Christian chiefs of Pomerania had not prevented him. They would not hear of such a valuable life being sacrificed. Some of his followers, inspired by his devotion, endeavoured to reach the place, but were driven back by furious tempests, and it was not until thirty years later (A.D. 1168) that this last fortress of Paganism in Europe fell, and its huge four-headed idol, Swantevit, which had been a terror for centuries, was hewn in pieces and committed to the flames.

In 1128 Otto returned to Bamberg, and spent the rest of his life in superintending the affairs of his diocese. But he was not unmindful of the churches which he had founded, nor of the converts whom he had won. He kept up a loving intercourse with them to the end of his life, and one of his last acts evinced his unfailing interest in their welfare. Having heard that some Pomeranian Christians had been taken captives by the heathen, he bought a quantity of valuable goods at Halle, and sent them to Pomerania, with instructions that part of them should be distributed amongst the chieftains, in order to secure their kindly offices, and part expended in paying for the ransom of the Christian captives. He died in A.D. 1139, leaving behind him, in a dark and ferocious age, substantial proofs of his success as a Christian missionary; affording a memorable illustration that truth and love can win their way where voluntary poverty and studied magnificence have failed to secure an entrance; and that consistency and charity are more influential than either the rags of the mendicant or the robes of the prelate.

VIII.

RAYMUND LULL, PHILOSOPHER, MISSIONARY, MARTYR.

A.D. 1291—1315.

"FOR two centuries the name of Raymund Lull was the best known, and perhaps the most influential, in Europe, but how few know anything about him now!" So writes one of our historians, and probably the greater number of those who read this brief sketch of his life and labours may have never heard of him before. Still he was a great man, and withal a missionary hero; all the greater, and all the more heroic, because he lived in the darkest of what may with justice be called the dark ages. His life and character were singular;—first a libertine, and then a saint; looked upon alternately as a fanatic and a philosopher; now dreaded as a heretic, and then reverenced as a devotee; poet and linguist, missionary and martyr, he was altogether the most remarkable man that stands out from the dark background of the thirteenth and fourteenth centuries.

His evangelistic labours moreover were mainly directed towards two classes, who had been long overlooked in the missionary efforts of the Church, namely, the Moslems and the Jews. It is true that the preaching friars, who started into existence in the early part of the thirteenth century, had renounced the idea of solitary life in the monasteries, and gone forth amongst the masses: and to Saracens, Moors, and Hebrews, as well as to heathens and professing Christians, they had carried such a gospel as they knew; but the labours of Raymund Lull were of a purer and more systematic kind; and though he caught some portion of his zeal from the example of the mendicant orders, he far outshone them in the clearness of his teaching and the far-sightedness of his arrangements.

He was born A.D. 1236, at Palma, in the

island of Majorca, and like several of the missionaries whom we have already described, was of noble birth. At an early age he was introduced at court, and was advanced to the rank of seneschal. Up to his thirtieth year he lived a life of gaiety and dissipation. Gifted, courted, impassioned, he spent his time between the culture of the muses, the frivolities of gay companions, and the indulgence of sensual passions. In after-life he wrote a work on "The Contemplation of God," and in it he laments this period of his worse than wasted life. "I see, O Lord," he writes, "that the trees every year bring forth flowers and fruits by which men are refreshed and nourished, but it is not so with me, a sinner. For thirty years I have borne no fruit in the world; yea, rather, I have injured my neighbours and friends. If therefore the tree which is destitute of reason brings forth more fruit than I have done, I must be deeply ashamed, and acknowledge my great guilt."

Such was the man whom Divine grace

selected to be a herald of salvation! He was sitting one day upon his couch, and composing a poem upon the joys of guilty love, when suddenly he seemed to behold the person of the Redeemer hanging upon the cross. So deep was the impression, that he could compose no more. He endeavoured to return to his love-song again and again, but every time the impression rose up more vividly before him, and he cast aside his guilty theme under the deep conviction that Christ was calling him to purer and nobler work. But then the thought flashed across his mind, "How can I, who am so impure, enter upon a holier life?" Night after night he lay awake in doubt and despair, and then the thought arose within him, "Christ is meek and merciful, and He invites all to come unto Him, and has promised that He will in no wise cast them out." This was the turning-point of his life: he embraced the proferred mercy, and resolved to dedicate himself henceforth to the service of the Lord.

His thoughts turned to the Saracens,

as being most in need of the Gospel of Christ. His father had served in the wars against them. He knew full well how the chivalry of Europe had failed to subjugate them. He had seen how the spirit of the Crusades had reacted upon the Church, and stirred up a kind of ecclesiastical militia to propagate the faith by the force of arms instead of by the power of love. He knew full well how the "Knights of the Sword" had brought dishonour upon Christianity by their cruelties and coercions. "I see many knights," he says, "crossing the sea to the Holy Land, and they imagine that they shall conquer it by force of arms, but at last they are all driven away without accomplishing their object; hence it appears to me that the Holy Land can be won in no other way than as Thou, O Lord Christ, and Thy Apostles won it—by love, by prayer, by shedding of tears and blood." And again, "The Holy Sepulchre and the Holy Land can be won back far more effectually by proclaiming the word of truth than by force of arms."

It occurred to him that he should write a book in order to prove the truth of Christianity; but then a difficulty presented itself: Of what use would such a volume be to the Saracens, who understood no language but Arabic? It was in pondering over this difficulty that he conceived the idea of applying to the pope and the princes of Christendom to found institutions for teaching foreign languages, that so the Gospel might be spread more widely through the world. He felt that linguistic study should be made subservient to the work of God; and amidst many discouragements and disappointments in high places, he never ceased to push his project, until, at the Council of Vienne, A.D. 1311, he obtained a degree that professorships of oriental languages should be founded in the universities of Paris, Oxford, and Salamanca, and in all cities where the papal court was held. He had already prevailed on the king of the Balearic Islands to found a monastery in Majorca, where thirteen students were to be instructed in Arabic, and trained in the Mahommedan controversy.

He had resolved to dedicate his own personal exertions to missionary labour; but for a time old habits regained their ascendancy, and all higher aspirations seemed to be quenched within him. It was at this crisis of his life that he heard a sermon on " renunciation of the world." It was preached by a Franciscan bishop, who told the thrilling story of the founder of his order, and how the gay soldier of fortune, brought down to the gates of the grave, had learned to see the things of time in the light of eternity, and to become the " Spouse of Poverty" and the servant of the cross. This sermon rekindled his missionary ardour. He sold his property, made provision for his wife and children, and left his home, with the intention of never returning to it again.

Soon afterwards we find him engaged in the study of Arabic. He bought a Saracen slave to teach him the language, and occupied himself for years in the acquisition of it. He then applied himself to construct a system of philosophy which might supersede the dialectics of the schoolmen, and harmonize the domains of science and theology. This conception he embodied in his "Ars Generalis," or, as it was long called, after its author, "The Lullian Art." He spent nine years in preparing it and lecturing on it. It was subtle, mystical, acute, and, in view of our modern philosophy, both useless and extravagant; but it was the product of a deep thinker, who had an enthusiastic hope of discovering a system of argumentation which would convince all men of the truth of the Christian faith.

Successive visits to Rome convinced him that he need not look for much aid or countenance in that quarter for his missionary projects; so he resolved to start upon the enterprise himself, and selected the Moslem population of Northern Africa as his field of labour. Repairing to Genoa in A.D. 1287, he engaged a passage to that dark continent, which in our own day has become once more the scene of so much

Christian effort. Great expectations were awakened among the Genoese by such an enterprise, undertaken by a man whose strange history and increasing fame had attracted universal attention. The ship was in the harbour; Lull's books were on board; everything was ready for the voyage; but, alas for poor human nature! his imagination conjured up all the terrors which might await him amongst the infidels; his heart quailed before the prospect, and he let the ship sail without him.

Scarcely was the vessel outside the harbour when he was visited with the keenest remorse for the scandal which he had brought upon religion, and the recreant faithlessness which he had displayed towards his plighted vows. A dreadful fever was the result of this mental conflict; but whilst in this agitated and prostrate state he heard of another ship which was just starting for Tunis, and he insisted upon being put on board. His friends, seeing that he was more dead than alive, and dreading the consequences of a voyage while he was in such a condition, brought him back; but he got no rest for his mind, and no alleviation for his illness. Another ship was about to sail, and no entreaties could now detain him. He insisted upon being placed on board, and no sooner had the ship weighed anchor than he began to revive. He felt he was now in the path of duty, and with returning peace of mind his bodily health came back. Like another Jonah, he had fled from God, but like him had been brought back to his forsaken work.

Arrived in Tunis, Raymund invited the Mahommedan literati to a public conference, and explained to them that he wished to institute a comparison between their religion and his own; and that if he found that they had stronger reasons on their side than he had on his, he would embrace the Moslem faith. The Mahommedan doctors flocked around him in great numbers, feeling sure of an easy victory; but after refuting their arguments in favour of their creed, he proceeded to show (and it was a favourite theme of his) that the doctrine of the Trinity, and the incarnation of the Son of God, were the only means of harmonizing the Divine attributes. From this he went on to show the conformity of Christianity to the dictates of reason, and then pressed home upon his hearers the acceptance of the Gospel message. He was, *par excellence*, "the philosophic missionary."

His argument must have been weighty, though not convincing; for one of the learned Saracens informed the king that their faith was in danger through Raymund's preaching, and succeeded in having him cast into prison and condemned to death. Another doctor, however, less prejudiced, espoused his cause, and declared that a man of such intellectual ability and heroic zeal as Lull should be honoured for his endeavours to spread the religion which he believed to be true, and that if any Mussulman had done so amongst the Christians he would have deserved the highest praise. This saved our missionary from death, but not from banishment. He was put on board the vessel in which he had arrived, and informed that if ever he visited Tunis again he should be stoned to death. He contrived, however, secretly to get on board another vessel, and lingered for three months in the harbour, with the hope of obtaining access to the city. During this period he commenced another of those philosophical treatises which made his name so famous in the fourteenth and fifteenth centuries.

We next find him at Naples, delivering lectures on his favourite system of philosophy. Then we find him again in Majorca, endeavouring to win the Saracens and Jews to the faith of Christ; then we follow him to the island of Cyprus, where he preached the Gospel; then we track him to Armenia, where he exerted himself to bring back various schismatics of the Eastern Church to orthodox doctrine; and all this labour and all these journeys he undertook with only one companion of his toil—unaided by the rich, unpatronised and unprotected by the great. Having spent ten years in varied labours and various climes, he returned to Europe, composed several important treatises, and lectured with applause in the Universities of France and Italy.

But Africa and the Saracens had possession of his heart. In A.D. 1307 he was once more beyond the Mediterranean, and preaching to the people of Buggia in the Arabic tongue, which was now as familiar to him as his own. Openly and publicly he proclaimed to them that the religion of Christ was true, and that of their prophet false. Many a hand was lifted up to stone him; but a mufti hurried him away, and asked him how he could be so infatuated as to expose his life to such certain peril. He replied, "Death has no terrors for a sincere servant of Christ, who is endeavouring to bring souls to the knowledge of the truth." Imprisonment, however, was his lot. For a year and a half he lay in a dark dungeon at Buggia, and meantime honours, riches, wives were offered to him if he would renounce his faith. To all such proffers he replied, "I also will promise you wealth, and honour, and everlasting life, if you will renounce your false prophet, and believe in the Lord Jesus Christ."

At length he was banished from the country, and was shipwrecked not far from Pisa. Many of his fellow-passengers were drowned, and he himself escaped with the loss of all his books and property. He was now an old man, and had won many an admirer on account of his labours, his learning, and his zeal. One might think that seventy winters had chilled the missionary ardour in his breast; but he reviews the past with cheerfulness, and looks to the future with undaunted hope. "Once," he writes, "I was rich; I had a wife and children; I led a worldly life. All these I cheerfully resigned for the sake of promoting the common good, and diffusing abroad the holy faith. I learned Arabic; I have gone abroad several times to preach the Gospel to the Saracens; I have, for the sake of the faith, been cast into prison; I have been scourged; I have laboured during forty-five years to win over the shepherds of the Church and the princes of Europe to the common good of Christendom. Now I am old and poor; but still I am intent on the same object, and I will persevere in it until death, if the Lord permit."

Such language reminds one of the great Apostle of the Gentiles, and we cannot doubt that, as the love of Christ constrained St. Paul, so it constrained this grand old man. Hear how he writes: "As the needle by nature turns to the north when it is touched by the magnet, so it is fitting that Thy servant should turn to Thee, since out of love to him Thou hast endured such pains and sufferings." And again: "I have sought Thee on the crucifix, and my bodily eyes could not find Thee there. I have sought Thee with the eyes of my soul, and as soon as I found Thee my heart grew warm with the glow of Thy love, and my eyes began to shed tears, and my mouth to praise Thee." It was no wonder that one who knew such love as this should desire to spend and be spent for the Master's sake; and so he says, "Men are wont to die, O Lord, of old age, because their natural warmth fails, and because there is excess of cold. Thus, if it be Thy will, Thy servant would not die. He would rather die in the glow of love, even as Thou wert willing to die for him."

And the Lord granted him that which he desired. He crossed over to Africa once more, on the 14th of August, 1314, and landed again at Buggia. He was now nearly eighty years of age, but "his eye was not dim, nor his natural force abated." Here he laboured secretly and quietly for a time amongst the little flock which he had gathered for Christ during his former visit, confirming their faith, and building them up in the knowledge of God. But his thirst for martyrdom was too strong to be repressed. It was the weakness of a great mind. He stood forth publicly once more, and declared to the astonished Saracens that he was the man whom they had banished from their shores. He exhorted them to renounce their errors, and predicted the judgments of the Almighty if they persisted in their unbelief.

The Saracens fell upon him in fury. He was dragged out of the city, and by the king's command was stoned to death. One account says that some merchants from Majorca obtained permission to remove his corpse, and that they found some sparks of life in him, which soon expired. The other account informs us that they removed the martyr's body from its stony coverlet, and carried it back to his native land. So died Raymund Lull on the 30th of June, 1315. He deserves to be had in remembrance as one of those " of whom the world was not worthy." He stood almost alone as a shining light in an age of surpassing darkness. He realized with wonderful fore cast some of the great necessities of the missionary enterprise, and more especially of linguistic culture. He consecrated his science and himself to the service of religion. He was the pioneer in far distant times of the Moffats and Livingstones and Krapfs, who in our own day have lived and died for Africa. He was one of the first to direct the attention of the Church of Christ to the long-neglected claims of the Moslem and the Jew; and now, when his philosophy is forgotten, and his dialectics are replaced by nobler and clearer systems of knowledge and instruction, we turn with admiration to the fervour of his love and the vigour of his faith.

IX.

FRANCIS XAVIER, MISSIONARY TO THE INDIES AND JAPAN.

A.D. 1541—1552.

THE Reformation of the sixteenth century inaugurated a new era of missionary enterprise. It was scarcely to be expected that the reformed churches, struggling for liberty and even for existence at home, could enter at once upon the foreign field. The history of their missions is of a somewhat later date, and will come under consideration hereafter; but the Church of Rome seemed determined to make up, if possible, for her losses in Europe by attempting new conquests in the East; and to this end she employed the new and powerful order of the Jesuits, which had sprung into existence amidst the conflicts of these times.

However we may disapprove of the character and conduct of these missions, it is impossible to leave them out of account in such a work as the present; and for the same reasons that lead us to notice them we cannot refrain from sketching the history of by far the most remarkable man who was concerned in this movement; we mean Francis Xavier, commonly called by Romish writers, "the Apostle of the Indies."

In placing him amongst the "Heroes of the Mission Field," we neither endorse his peculiar religious dogmas nor give our approbation to all his methods for propagating them. As will be seen in the sequel, there was much in both which must be strongly condemned; but at the same time we cannot withhold our admiration, not only of his zeal, energy, and self-devotion, but, notwithstanding all his darkness and defects, his undeniable love to the great Master Whom he endeavoured to honour and to serve. Moreover we must distinguish between the man as he really was and those exaggerated and absurd portraits of him which have been drawn by credulous and superstitious hands. Perhaps there is no missionary who has left us such ample materials as he has done, in his own letters, for drawing up a history both of his character and work; and one cannot imagine a greater contrast than "Xavier" as described by his own pen and "Xavier" as portrayed in the legendary histories which in after years pretended to set forth his claims. As a late writer has well said, "in the sober realities of his history there is enough to entitle him to a high rank in the roll of self-devoted philanthropists. But his eulogists claim for him the title of a Christian hero upon grounds which are untenable."

We need not dwell upon the miraculous powers, some of them most puerile and absurd, which have been attributed to him. It would be easy to show, if this were the place to do it, that these claims cannot be sustained upon rational grounds, and are contradicted by the accredited statements which have come to us from under his own hand.

For example, the more than pentecostal gift of tongues, by which it is said that he not only spake in languages which he had never learned, but so spake that people of different tongues all understood him at one and the same moment, is flatly contradicted by his own repeated confession, that one of his great difficulties consisted in his ignorance of the languages of the people amongst whom he went, and his dependence upon native interpreters who were liable to mistake his meaning.

But we turn from fictions to the broad facts which can be relied upon concerning this remarkable man. He was born in the ancestral castle of Xaviere, upon the Spanish slopes of the Pyrenees, on the 7th of April, 1506, and like many of the missionaries whose histories we have already sketched, he belonged both by paternal and maternal descent to ancient and honourable families. All his elder brothers were trained to the profession of arms; but Francis, the youngest of a large family, showed an early love of study, mingled with that love of adventure and romance which were to be ultimately devoted to higher ends. At seventeen he was sent to the University of Paris, where he became a distinguished student, and a still more distinguished professor of philosophy. His lecture-room was crowded by the *élite* of Parisian society; his eloquence, his beauty, and his learning attracted people from all quarters, and men bowed down before the inspiration of his genius as if in the presence of something almost divine.

It was at this time that he became acquainted with a man who was destined to exercise a magic spell, not only upon him, but upon many others—namely, Ignatius Loyola, the future general of the order of the Jesuits. It is remarkable that at first Xavier disliked Ignatius, and treated him with disdain. There is reason to believe that at this period of his life Xavier had come into contact with the opinions of the Reformers, and was not altogether uninfluenced by them; but eventually his whole nature came under the enchantment of his new acquaintance, and to the end of his life he never ceased to express the most unbounded admiration and respect for him. Indeed, Xavier was one of the memorable "seven" who in the crypt of St. Denis, at Montmarte, took the Vow of Dedication which gave rise to the famous "Society of Jesus;" and the whole of his missionary life was inspired by the ardour of his devotion to that community and its extraordinary founder.

It was to Palestine that Xavier and his companions first turned their eyes as a field of labour; but circumstances arose which directed their steps to the farther East. While he was staying with Ignatius at Rome and organizing the band of labourers who were to go forth for new conquests on its behalf, an application was made to the Pope by John III. of Portugal for some able and devoted missionaries to preach in his Indian dominions. The result of the application was that Xavier and another of the order were selected for the enterprise, and within a few days they were on the road to

Lisbon, in company with the ambassador. It is said that on the way thither he passed close by the castle of Xaviere, and that though pressed by the ambassador to visit it and to see his aged mother, Xavier declined to do so. If the story be true, it shows to what mistaken lengths the vow of self-sacrifice was already leading the young neophyte; but at the same time it manifests the entire determination with which he devoted himself to his work.

After being detained about a year in Lisbon, the missionary and his party sailed in April, 1541, in company with the king's new viceroy, with a fleet of six splendid ships, and loaded with every honour and dignity that royal or ecclesiastical power could confer upon them. Indeed, this overshadowing by human authority, and a consequent reliance upon it, proved to be the weak points in Xavier's mission. He was devoid of personal vanity, but he was too prone to lean upon an arm of flesh, and too little upon the power of divine truth; and, as we shall see in the sequel, this often proved a snare to him, and a real hindrance to his work.

Arrived in Goa, he soon found that his romantic dreams were to be rudely dissipated by the ungodly conduct of the Portuguese settlers, both clerical and lay. How could the heathen be evangelized while the representatives of Christianity in their midst were a disgrace to the very name they bore? For five months he devoted himself to the work of reformation. His days were spent in preaching, in catechizing the young, in visiting the hospitals. His zeal and piety were something new, and he seems to have won admiration and respect, and, what was far better, to have accomplished a manifest improvement in the conduct and morals of the community.

But his heart yearned after work of a more directly missionary kind, and he looked around upon the vast expanse of heathendom about him to see where he should commence. But here at the outset he was hampered by political connections. The viceroy had a favourite project: it was to Christianize or rather to re-Christianize the pearl-fishers of the Comorin coast, and, still more, to secure the monopoly of the pearl fishery for his royal master. These fishermen had been won, at least nominally, to the Christian faith by the previous labour of Michael Vas, but they possessed little of Christianity except the name. This mention of a previous labourer in India reminds us that there were many such before the days of Xavier, and that consequently he cannot in any exact sense be considered as the apostle of that country. And so Francis Xavier started for his first field of missionary labour. We have his own account of his work. He began by translating the Creed, the Lord's Prayer, the Ten Commandments, and the Ave Maria into the vernacular, and committing them to memory. Then, with bell in hand, he went forth through the villages, and summoned large congregations, attracting children especially by his kind words and gentle looks. To these he recited the translations, and after each article of the creed he asked them whether they believed. On their assent, he gave a short exhortation and then and there baptized them. With such a facile system, we do not wonder to hear him say, "It often happens to me that my hands fail through the fatigue of baptizing, for I have baptized a whole village in a single day; and often by repeating so frequently the creed and other things, my voice and strength have failed me." How little his catechumens understood may be gathered from a letter of Xavier to his friend Mansilla, in which he says that they had mistranslated the first word of the creed, and that instead of the word "I believe" (*credo*), they had been using the expression "I will" (*volo*).

Xavier's custom of baptizing infants whose parents were still heathen (a custom always reprobated by the early Church) was another example of the way in which both then and since the statistics of Romish missions have been swelled. Xavier boasts that he baptized more than a thousand infants within twelve months, and speaks of them as gone up to heaven to be his intercessors! But he soon tired of this kind of work, and longed to convert kings and princes. He was attracted to the kingdom of Travancore, where he hoped to gain its powerful sovereign, and so ensure great successes amongst his subjects.

If we are to take a passage in one of his letters as authentic, he made 10,000 converts in this kingdom within a single month; but there is strong reason to believe that the passage is not genuine; and even if it were, the mode of making them, as described already (*feci christianos*), must be taken into account. They were made by means of an unknown language, and by the unreliable help of a native interpreter, and with the smallest possible amount of instruction. How little value Xavier himself finally set upon the results of such labours may be gathered from his own statement—" If you will, in imagination, search through India, you will find that few reach heaven, either of whites or blacks, except those who depart this life under fourteen years of age, with their baptismal innocence still upon them." The Abbé Dubois has given us a like melancholy picture of the transitory effects produced by Xavier's mission in India. Indeed, he does not hesitate to say of Xavier, that "being entirely disheartened by the invincible obstacles he everywhere met in his apostolic career, and by the apparent impossibility of making real converts, he left the country in disgust."

It is important to bear all this in mind when estimating the results achieved by Xavier. They are not the kind of results which would satisfy us in any case, nor could we expect more permanent ones from the teaching which led to them; but all this need not hinder us from admiring the energy and self-denial with which he pursued his labours, or the generous, noble, and loving disposition which he so undeniably displayed. In these respects we may repeat what a Protestant historian (Baldeus) has said in his "History of the Indies"—"Oh that it had pleased God that, being what you were, you had been, or might have been, one of us!"

Xavier quitted India after three years of labour, but with a feeling akin to mortification and despair. The king of Jaffnapatam had made cruel ravages upon the Christians of Ceylon, and Xavier had endeavoured to coerce him by the power of the sword of Portugal; but this reliance upon the "arm of flesh" proved unavailing, and the missionary turned his eyes to Macassar and the islands of the Indian Archipelago, from which he had heard exciting news, and where he hoped to win great successes. He sailed for Macassar in 1545, and soon arrived at Malacca. Here, as in other places, he took up his residence in the hospital, and spent his time in doing good both amongst the sick and in the city; but with an inconstancy which seemed peculiar to him, he abandoned his project of going to Macassar, and started for Amboyna, the Moluccas and Mauriciæ, all of which he visited in turn, and in each of which he laboured, sometimes at the risk of life, often amidst the want of all things, and always with a spirit of self-sacrifice and earnest devotion. His mission in these regions lasted from 1545 to 1548.

His letters to Europe at this period are filled with the most ecstatic accounts of his labours and sensations, and yet at the very same period he writes to his fellow-labourers in tones of depression and disappointment. We are not to conclude from this that Xavier was double-tongued or deceitful. He was a man of very emotional character and quick transitions of feeling. His letters to his friends reflect the sorrow and pain which sprang up in his daily work; whilst his more elaborate reports, written at lengthened intervals, give the more trustful confidence of his personal faith in God. But he lacked that confidence in the power of the Gospel, and indeed that spiritual knowledge of it, which would have made him "steadfast and immovable." Nothing more fully evinces this sad defect in Xavier's views of divine truth than his proposal to the king of

Portugal, that in future the work of missions should be confided to the civil authorities! He gravely tells the king, in a letter dated 20th January, 1548, that this is the only remedy against the failure of missions, and counsels the king to hold the viceroys and governors personally responsible for the success of the missions in their different districts, and to " punish the governor of any town or province in which few neophytes are added to our holy Church," and he proposes that this punishment should extend to " close imprisonment for many years, and that all his goods and possessions shall be sold and devoted to works of charity!"

We do not marvel after this that India and the Spice Islands were forsaken. And now Japan presented a new and attractive field to the enterprising but disappointed missionary. The providence of God had brought a native of that country, named Anger, into contact with Xavier. The missionary appears to have been blessed to him; and Anger, who at his baptism took the name of "Paul of the holy faith," soon interested his instructor in the spiritual wants of his countrymen. Xavier's name will ever be honourably associated with the introduction of Christianity into Japan; and if his followers in that mission had been actuated in all respects by the same spirit which influenced him, we probably would never have read of the terrible outburst of persecution which a century afterwards destroyed so many valuable lives (they are reckoned at 37,000), and shut up the country until our own times against the re-admission of Christian missionaries. It was in 1549 that he and his companions sailed in a Chinese junk to the port of Cangoxima. His ignorance of the language operated as a serious hindrance to his work; but still he seems to have gained a hearing for Christianity, and to have won considerable numbers of the Japanese to the reception of it. There is something heroic in the simple story of his privations and difficulties, as, in the depth of winter, thinly clad and barefoot, he made his two months' journey to the capital, Meaco, through snow-drifts and mountain torrents.

But the old diplomatic attractions once more came into play. The king of Bungo, who had given a very favourable reception to Xavier, though unwilling to become a Christian, was anxious to establish commercial relations with Portugal. The missionary, always too anxious to fall back upon royal support, soon arranged to leave Japan, in company with a native ambassador and two Japanese Christians, in order to carry out these political arrangements. Thus closed his two and a half years' mission in that interesting land. He bequeathed it to others; but it is lamentable to tell how, after existing for ninety years, the mission was extinguished in blood, and how by a terrible Nemesis it was brought to an end by political power—the very power upon which Xavier and his followers had so constantly relied. Intercepted letters informed the Emperor that the teachers of the new religion intended to raise sedition against him. A terrible persecution ensued, in which thousands endured death rather than renounce their Christianity; and above the vast grave in which the Japanese martyrs were interred, these awful words were written: "So long as the sun shall warm the earth, let no Christians be so bold as to come to Japan, and let all know that the king of Spain himself, or the Christian's God, or the great God of all, if he violate this command, shall pay the forfeit with his head."

It was while Xavier was in Japan that he conceived the idea of opening a mission to China. Many circumstances led him in this direction: his own restlessness and romance of spirit; the high esteem in which the Chinese were held by the people of Japan; and the hope that if the former could be won, the latter would soon follow; and moreover there was then the report (fully verified in our own day) that there were Jews in the interior of China; this report recalled Xavier's early dreams about Palestine, and led him to imagine that a way might be opened to him from the Celestial Empire to Jerusalem itself.

In a letter from Goa, April 10th, 1552, he thus announces his intentions to the king of Portugal: "I go from hence in five days to Malacca, with a brother of our society, James Pereira, an envoy to the king of China. We carry with us many precious gifts to the king, which Pereira has bought, partly by royal funds and partly by his own. We carry also a precious gift such as I doubt whether ever any king sent to a king within the memory of man —namely, the Gospel of Jesus Christ, which, if the king of China knows its value, he will place far above all his treasures, however great." These were noble words, but the project was destined to end in disappointment. Arrived at Malacca, Xavier proposed a "legation" to China, hoping by that means to secure admission to a land which it would be otherwise death to enter. He found, however, that the new governor was adverse to his enterprise, and with a strange admixture of the pontifical legate and the devoted missionary, he forthwith assigned the governor to excommunication in the severest language, and resolved to start alone upon the perilous expedition. He took shipping in the *Santa Cruz*, and was soon off the coast of China, accompanied only by a native interpreter and a young Indian.

There is something very sublime in the last days of the earnest but baffled missionary, as he stands upon the barren island of Sancian, and looks in vain for admission through the closed doors of the Celestial Empire. Again and again he was heard to exclaim, "O rock, rock, when wilt thou open?" He tried by means of vast bribes (it was a very questionable effort) to induce some of the Chinese, at the risk of their lives, to smuggle him on shore, but the attempt ended in failure. Then fever seized him as he lay in his rude hut, constructed of stakes and branches, upon the sandy beach, and ever and anon, amid his ravings, his heart gave utterance to his faith: "Deus meus et omnia." He was only forty-six; his hair was white, not with age, but with constant toil and suffering; his noble face was hectic with the flush of fever; his long thin hands were emaciated by disease. And there, far away from companionship and sympathy, after ten such years of toil and labour as few men have ever endured, he breathed out his life on the 2nd of December, 1552, in these memorable words, " In te, Domine, speravi ; non confunda, inæternum."

Rome has beatified and canonized Francis Xavier, and she has done so upon grounds which will not bear investigation; she has surrounded his memory with legends and extravagances which in no way add to his true honour; and she has claimed for him powers and successes which are repudiated by his own pen. But he was nevertheless the noblest and most gifted of her missionaries. He had his faults and failings; but he never defiled himself by frauds and falsehoods, like those which marked the conduct of so many of his successors in India, and which grew at length to such a pitch of enormity that they called forth papal condemnation. We can do justice to his integrity and zeal, whilst conscious of his spiritual errors and defective teaching; and we can applaud and recommend his earnestness and devotedness, whilst guarding ourselves and others against those earthly confidences which hindered and marred his work.

Perhaps no higher testimony can be borne to his character than that reflected from his personal piety, as manifested in the words of his own beautiful hymn:—

> O Deus! ego amo te,
> Nec amo te, ut salves me,
> Aut quia non amantes te
> Æterno punis igne.
> Tu, tu, mi Jesu, totum me
> Amplexus es in cruce:
> Tulisti clavos, lanceam,
> Multamque ignominiam,
> Innumeros dolores,
> Sudores et angores,
> Ac mortem, et hæc propter me,
> Ac pro me peccatore:
> Cui igitur non amem te,
> O Jesu, amantissime?
> Non ut in cælo salves me,
> Aut ne æternum damnes me,
> Nec præmii illius spe,

Sed sicut tu amasti me ;
Sic amo et amabo te,
Solum quia Rex meus es,
Et solum quia Deus es.

The following translation of it will be acceptable to English readers:—

My God, I love Thee, not because
   I hope for heav'n thereby ;
Nor yet that they who love Thee not
   Must burn eternally.
Thou, O my Jesus, Thou didst me
   Upon the cross embrace ;
For me didst bear the nails and spear,
   And manifold disgrace ;
And griefs and torments numberless,
   And sweat of agony :
Even death itself ; and all for one
   Who was Thine enemy.
Then why, O blessed Jesu Christ,
   Should I not love Thee well ?
Not for the sake of winning heav'n,
   Or of escaping hell :
Not with the hope of gaining aught,
   Nor seeking a reward ;
But as Thyself hast lov'd me,
   O ever-loving Lord ,
E'en so I love Thee, and will love,
   And in Thy praise will sing ;
Because Thou art my Lord, and God,
   And my Eternal King !

X.

ELIOT, THE APOSTLE OF THE RED INDIANS.

A.D 1646—1690.

WE now enter upon the era of Protestant missions. The Reformed Churches had found it difficult at the outset of their new career to attend to missionary work amongst the heathen. They were not, however, entirely forgetful of this sacred duty. In 1555, a few years after the death of Xavier, a mission had been organized by Calvin and the Church of Geneva, which sent out fourteen missionaries to Brazil, in company with an expedition which had been set on foot by the famous Admiral Coligni. This expedition failed in consequence of the treachery and apostasy of a knight of Malta, to whose charge it had been entrusted; the greater part of the colonists had to return home, and the rest were barbarously murdered by the Portuguese. In 1559 a mission was undertaken to Lapland, under the royal sanction of Gustavus Vasa, King of Sweden, and was perpetuated by those who came after with no small success. The remainder, however, of the sixteenth century was not fruitful in missionary enterprise, and we arrive at the middle of the seventeenth century before we come to any distinguished name upon the illustrious roll of modern missionaries.

It is here that we meet with the name of John Eliot, who, although declining for himself the modest title of "Evangelist of the Indians," has won by very general consent the higher title of their "Apostle." He was in every sense a remarkable man, and may be taken as a typical character amongst the Heroes of the Mission Field.

His mission took its rise out of the strange and in many respects deplorable events which drove the "Pilgrim Fathers" out of England, and led them to seek for liberty and toleration on the shores of

America. The colony had been founded about twelve years before Eliot went out to his exiled countrymen as spiritual instructor; and he was acting for some years in that capacity before it came into his heart to devote himself to the heathen tribes who were round about him.

He was born in 1604, and brought up by pious parents, of whom he spoke in after life with reverence and gratitude. He received a university education at Cambridge, where he distinguished himself in theology and classics, and it is probable that he entered into holy orders; but it does not appear that he exercised any clerical functions in England. It would rather seem as if he had early imbibed the opinions of the Nonconformists of his day, for we find him assisting in the school of one Thomas Hooker, who from conscientious motives had retired from the ministry of the Church of England, and settled at Little Baddow, near Chelmsford. But it is to the credit of John Eliot that he did not carry any narrow or bitter spirit into his life-long work, but discharged it with a broad and Christian charity, and successfully resisted his co-religionists in their opposition to infant baptism and other ordinances of the Church from which he had been unhappily severed.

The earlier relations of the colonists with the Indian tribes were marked by considerable fairness and integrity; and the desire expressed in their foundation charter—that they should keep in view the conversion of the natives to the Christian faith—had not been altogether lost sight of; but nothing was done upon a definite or extensive scale until Eliot took it in hand. He had been fifteen years labouring amongst his fellow-emigrants at the village of Roxbury (now a suburb of the great city of Boston) when in 1646 he entered upon his arduous work amongst the Red Indians. For some years previously his sympathies had gone forth towards a race which, amidst all their degradation and superstition, have possessed so many noble and admirable qualities, that they have been designated "the born gentlemen of mankind." In addition to this, he had persuaded himself that they were a portion of the lost tribes of Israel; and to a man holding the peculiar views which distinguished the Pilgrim Fathers, who made the Jewish Commonwealth the model of their own State Government, this persuasion would supply a class of motives most sacred and influential.

His chief difficulty lay in the languages which he had to conquer. It has been well said of Eliot that he had "the gift of tongues;" but not in the sense in which it was vouchsafed to the Apostles, or in which, as we have seen, it has been attributed to Xavier. He possessed a marvellous power of mastering a foreign tongue, and he had to deal with languages so difficult, that, to use the words of the historian, "they must have been growing since Babel." What do our readers think of

" Kummogokdonattoottammoctiteaongannunnonash,"

which was the nearest correlative to "catechism"? or how do they estimate the labour which had to reduce to writing a language containing such polysyllabic words—a language for which there was no alphabet, grammar, or vocabulary; and one moreover which contained no equivalents for the fundamental ideas which it was the main object of the Christian missionary to set forth?

"I found out," says Eliot, "a pregnant-witted man, who pretty well understood our language: him I made my interpreter. By his help I translated the Commandments, the Lord's Prayer, and many texts of Scripture; also I compiled both exhortations and prayers by his help. I diligently marked the difference of their grammar from ours; and when I found the way of them, I would pursue a word, a noun, a verb, through all variations I could think of." Such is the simple unostentatious way in which this great missionary records what must have been a gigantic labour.

It was on the 28th of October, 1646, that he made his first use of this laborious acquisition. He met the Indians, by appointment, some five miles from Roxbury, and was introduced to them by Waban, an influential man amongst his tribe, who led Eliot to the wigwam where the natives were assembled in large numbers. After a brief prayer, in which he sought help from heaven, he preached for a quarter of an hour upon Ezekiel's "vision of dry bones," and the breath of God quickening them. His hearers were greatly touched by what they heard; and Waban, whose name, by a curious coincidence, was "breath" or "wind," was specially attracted, and afterwards became a most useful helper to the missionary. After preaching, Eliot always encouraged his hearers to ask questions, and then did his best to answer them. Amongst the questions put to him he records the following:—"How can Indians come to know God?" "Can God understand prayer in the Indian tongue?" "Were Englishmen ever as ignorant of Jesus Christ as the Indians?" "Whether it were not too late for them to repent and seek after

God?" These questions indicate how fully the Indians were taking in the truths which they were being taught, and Eliot's mode of thus dealing with his hearers contrasts favourably with the rash and rapid manner in which converts were instructed and admitted to baptism by Xavier and other missionaries.

Eliot held successive meetings of this kind with the natives; and such was his success, that the *powows*, or medicine-men, took the alarm, and did their best to hinder the labour of the missionary. It was at this juncture Waban espoused their cause, and repeated to his countrymen the lessons he had learned from the white man. About the same time another Indian, named Wampas, brought his son and other children to be instructed in the Christian religion, and this example was soon followed by other natives, so that Eliot found his hands full, and had to devote himself to the twofold work of education and of preaching.

He soon found that, owing to the roving

habits of the Indians, little could be effectually done for their civilization; so he resolved upon gathering them into settled communities, and began by building a town where they might learn the simple arts of life, and receive constant instruction for themselves and their children. This town was called Nonanetum (or *gladness*), and it soon became the centre of Christian influence. Polygamy was discontinued; agriculture was introduced; the wild habits of former times were exchanged for the decencies of civilized life; one Christian village after another rose in the wilderness, and in one instance, that of "Concord," the movement originated with the Indians themselves. The experience gathered from various quarters has shown that, in the commencement of a mission, such a mode of procedure is often not only desirable, but necessary; and that at the same time this system of pupilage should be gradually relaxed, and the converts accustomed to the exercise of that manly Christianity which can encounter the shocks and conflicts of the world in which it has to live, and which it is intended to influence and transform. Eliot's use of the system was both necessary and successful.

In 1674 there were no fewer than seven towns of praying Indians, with their "seven churches," and a population of about eleven hundred souls. The Lord's-day was piously observed, and large congregations assembled at the sound of a drum to praise and worship the true God. Some of the influential Sachems (or chiefs) joined the movement, and one of them, named Papassaconnoway, and his sons, gave great help to the missionary. The speech of one chief is worth recording. He said: "I have all my days been paddling in an old canoe, and now you exhort me to leave my old canoe, which I have been hitherto unwilling to do; but now I yield myself to your advice, and enter into a new canoe, and do engage myself to pray henceforth to God alone." But other chiefs violently opposed the missionary, and he was sometimes in peril of his life at their hands. By this time Eliot had obtained the valuable help of such men as Cotton and Mayhew from England. He had also secured the aid of pious mechanics and labourers to instruct the natives; but his work and theirs had often to be carried on amidst much difficulty and hardship. Speaking of one of his itinerations, he says, "I have not been dry night nor day from the third day of the week unto the sixth, but so travelled, and at night pulled off my boots, wrung my stockings, and on with them again, and so continue. But God steps in and helps. I have considered the word of God in 2 Tim. ii. 3 : 'Endure hardship as a good soldier of Jesus Christ.' "

Eliot was distinguished by great perseverance, unfailing cheerfulness, and good common sense; but that which made him mighty was his spirit of love and his spirit of prayer. Even the New Englanders were not free from quarrels, but the gentleness of the good missionary acted like magic, and often dissipated their contentions. "He was ready," as his biographer quaintly expresses it, "to ring a loud curfew-bell whenever he saw the fire of animosity." And he carried this spirit into his dealings with the heathen, and won them to Christ by the power of love. As for prayer, it was the very breath which he breathed. He set apart whole days for prayer when any special work was to be done, and he never undertook the most ordinary duty without asking the Divine blessing. "Let us pray," was his usual salutation when entering the house of any of his friends, and his invariable address when about to leave it. "Pray, pray, pray!" these were the earnest words which mingled with his last utterances upon a dying bed.

He carried a kind of divine simplicity about him. Careful about the wants of others, he seldom attended to his own. His wife once asked him, "Whose were those cattle that stood before his door?" But the good man's mind was taken up with Indian alphabets and vocabularies, and he did not know that they belonged to himself! His salary upon one occasion was tied up in a handkerchief; and the treasurer, knowing Eliot's disposition, put as many knots upon it as he could. On his way home he called upon a poor widow, and found her destitute. He tried to undo the knots, but finding them more troublesome than he anticipated, he handed the whole to his astonished parishioner, saying, "Here, take it; I believe the Lord intends that you should get it all!"

The sagacity of Eliot was proved in the measures which he took to render his work abiding. Not content with laborious itinerations in which he followed the Indians to their hunting-grounds, and sought them out at their various fishing-stations, he established schools for the education of their children and a college for the training of a native ministry. Roxbury, in proportion to its size, sent out more scholars from its school, founded by Eliot, than any community in New England; and the famous college of Harvard owes not a little of its fame to the labours of this devoted missionary. His zeal and energy soon bore fruit in other parts of the new colonies, so much so that in 1687 Eliot tells us of four-and-twenty Indian preachers, besides four English ministers, who could address the people in their native tongue. He himself had five sons, all of whom he devoted to the work of the ministry. Two of them died young, two others were distinguished as evangelists, and the youngest assisted him in his declining years, but was called to his reward before his father. On being asked how he could bear up under the loss of so many of his children, Eliot replied, "It was my desire that they should have served God on earth; but if God chose rather that they should serve Him in heaven, I have nothing to object to it. His will be done."

He translated several important volumes into the Indian tongue; but his great work was the Mohegan version of the Holy Scriptures. In 1661 he had finished his translation of the New Testament, and, with the aid of the Corporation for Propagating the Gospel in New England (then lately revived under the presidency of the famous Robert Boyle), he printed fifteen hundred copies under the title of " Wusku Wuttustamentum Nut Lordumun Jesus Christ Nuppoquohwussuaeneumun." It may be observed, in recording this strange title, that he anticipated and settled for himself the lengthened controversy which has since arisen amongst missionaries as to the proper equivalents for such words as Lord, Christ, God, etc. Eliot preferred to use words which were new to the heathen, rather than run the risk of adopting expressions of theirs which were contaminated by their false systems of belief, and might therefore convey wrong impressions when used in connection with Christian truth. Three years afterwards he completed the translation of the Old Testament, and it is said that the whole of his MS. was written with a single pen ! It was the first Bible ever printed in America, and although in its day it did its blessed work, it is a sad reflection that it is now only fit for a museum, and that there is not an individual alive that can understand a word of it. The encroachments of the colonists, and their injustice to the natives, led to an internecine strife, in which the white man vied in ferocity with the red man whom he had oppressed, and in the issue gave him the unhappy distinction of having extinguished as well as wronged the original possessor of the soil.

Even before Eliot's death this terrible conflict had cast its coming shadow upon his work. Philip, chief of the Paukunnawkuts, and son of the Sachem who had received the pilgrims so kindly upon their first landing from the *Mayflower*, took up arms in 1675, in defence of his tribe, and after a bitter and sanguinary contest was killed in battle. Many of the converts espoused the cause of the English, while the majority, as was natural, sided with their own countrymen, and thus exposed Eliot to undeserved obloquy at the hands of the settlers, and to suspicion from some of his own converts. When peace was at last restored, he found that utter desolation reigned in some of his once happy settlements, and that many of the inhabitants in the others were either slain or dispersed. But though "cast down" he was not "destroyed." At the age of seventy-two he went forth once more upon his labour of faith and love, to revive his work from amidst the overthrow; and his devotedness was rewarded with success. In 1680 he says, " Our praying Indians on the islands and on the mainland amount to some thousands." In 1686 he speaks of six churches of baptized natives in New England, besides eighteen assemblies of catechumens.

He was now more than eighty years of age, and was fast drawing near to his end. His fifty years of failing strength hindered him from engaging in active work; but like a grand old sentinel he still kept watch and ward over the Church of God, and did what he could to promote his Saviour's glory. He did not resign his pastoral charge at Roxbury until two years before his death, and one of his last ministerial acts was to gather into his own house some of the poor negroes who had been brought as slaves into the colony, and there to instruct them in the knowledge of the Redeemer. Thus did this noble missionary close his days. The lamp which had burned so brightly for more than half a century was dim, but its light was not extinguished. "I have lost everything," said he, when some one inquired after his health; "my understanding leaves me; my memory fails me; my utterance fails; but I thank God my charity holds out still. I find *that* rather grows than fails." He was eighty-six when, on the 20th May, 1690, he entered into rest. His last utterances were these: "Welcome joy!" "Lord, only let Thy work amongst the Indians live after my decease!" "Come, Lord, come!"

His prayer was heard, and his work lived after him; for God raised up faithful men to finish it. Five generations of the Mayhews laboured one after the other in that fruitful field; Hiacoomes, a native evangelist, and his equally devoted son, were distinguished for their successful labours; and although the tribes for whom they toiled and prayed have ceased to be, it is some consolation to reflect that ere they melted away like snow before the advance of the white man, they were visited by the Gospel missionary, and reclaimed from savagedom and superstition.

It was the example and success of Eliot that directed public attention to the neglected tribes of the Red Indians. Devoted missionaries have followed in his track. David Brainerd went to Albany in 1742, and died at the early age of thirty, after a brief life of patient hardship and enthusiastic zeal, during which he achieved great success. The Moravians, ever active and dovoted in missionary enterprise, have had their converts and their martyrs amongst the wilds and prairies of the red man ; and in later years the churches of England and of America have sent some of their noblest sons to the hunting grounds of the far West, and farther North, and raised up Christian communities in their remotest bounds. A better spirit, though with some sad exceptions, has of late years marked the intercourse of the whites with the Indian races. The waste and extinction which were so often the result of oppression and injustice have in some instances been checked, and it is said that in the case of the Mohawks, they have been replaced by progress and increase.

But ever foremost in the history of this blessed work must stand the distinguished name of Eliot, "the Apostle of the Red Indians," who, in a half-awakened age, arose to the great duty of missionary enterprise, and who, amidst surroundings which might have made him severe and narrow-minded, exhibited a most loving and catholic spirit. His character was distinguished by a sublime simplicity and cheerful perseverance. Baxter, who was no bad judge of character, says of him in one of his letters, "There was no man on earth whom I honoured above him." It would be difficult to say whether his physical or his mental labours were the more arduous. His wisdom and sagacity marked out the paths and methods in which modern missions have found it best to tread; and his temper and spirit have furnished a model which after ages will do well to imitate, but which they can scarcely hope to excel. The words which he inscribed at the end of his own Indian grammar afford the clue to his success, and may well furnish a motto to every Christian worker :—

"PRAYERS AND PAINS, THROUGH FAITH IN JESUS CHRIST, WILL DO ANYTHING."

XI.

HANS EGEDE, THE APOSTLE OF GREENLAND.

A.D. 1721—1758.

THERE was one portion of the world to which, for centuries, no missionary footsteps had been turned, but which was now to become the scene of a new and most heroic Christian enterprise. Greenland had been colonized soon after its discovery in the tenth century by the Norwegians, and for some time the colonists kept up communication with home, and both enjoyed and diffused the light of the Gospel in their distant settlements. But terrible vicissitudes befell them: the black death decimated their ranks; the savage Esquimaux assailed the remnant that survived, and soon all intercourse ceased between them and their native country. It was believed that what was called "the Western Colony" had entirely perished, but a lingering hope remained that some of "the Eastern Colony" might still survive. For centuries, however, the eastern coast had been rendered inaccessible by ice, and every thought of reaching it seemed to have been abandoned, when, towards the beginning of the eighteenth century, Hans Egede conceived the twofold design of discovering the lost colonies, and of preaching the Gospel of Christ to the heathen Greenlanders.

He was by birth a Norwegian, and received his education at Copenhagen. In 1707, at the early age of twenty-one, he was ordained a pastor of Vaagen in northern Norway, and soon afterwards married Gertrude Rask, a noble-minded woman, who was destined to exercise a wonderful influence on him, and upon the mission to which his life was subsequently devoted.

He had not been long married when some records concerning the ancient colonists of Greenland fell into his hands, and as he read them his mind was fired to search out their descendants, if any such remained, and restore to them the light of Christianity, which he feared by this time must have perished from their midst. Side by side with this purpose grew up the more practical, and, as it eventually proved, the more effectual desire of preaching to the natives. It soon became an enthusiasm that carried his whole soul before it; but like many another grand design, it had to encounter obstacles of every kind, which only served to swell the flood they endeavoured to arrest. Argument, ridicule, slander, were all tried against him in turn. He wrote to the Bishops of Bergen and Trondhjem, explaining his project, but received only a cold reply. It struck him that his project came with a bad grace, inasmuch as *he* did not volunteer to go upon the service, and therefore he offered himself for the work; but he honestly informs us that as it was wartime, and money was difficult to be had, he thought it probable that his offer would not be accepted. The reply of one of these bishops was rather peculiar. He said that " there was no doubt that Greenland was part of America, and could not be far from Cuba, where there was plenty of gold, and that doubtless those who went there would bring home vast riches."

Egede had proceeded thus far without even acquainting his wife with his intentions, and when at last she became aware of them, she joined with all his friends in steadfastly opposing them, and continued her determined opposition for six long years. Some local difficulties however arose; a misunderstanding with a neighbouring clergyman led to what Egede graphically describes as "fishing in troubled waters;" the husband and wife betook themselves to united prayer for Divine guidance, and the result was that she became more enthusiastic than her partner, and from that day onward was the good angel of his missionary life.

He removed with his family to Copenhagen, in the hope of inducing the king of Denmark and the merchants of that city to undertake a mission, partly commercial, partly evangelistic, to the shores of Greenland. But everything seemed to baffle his endeavours. Reports had reached the capital that a ship had been wrecked on the inhospitable coast, and that the crew had been killed and eaten by the cannibal inhabitants. War moreover had brought its terrors and distress upon the nation, and men were unwilling or unable to supply the means for what was considered by most a romantic and hazardous experiment.

Thirteen tedious years were spent by Hans Egede in all kinds of fruitless appeals and negotiations, but his unwavering faith still sustained him. At length Frederick IV., who was personally favourable to missions, was induced to sanction the enterprise. Six thousand rix-dollars were raised by the solicitations of the missionary, and three hundred were his own personal gift. The king allowed Hans Egede three hundred dollars a year, and appointed him leader of the expedition, and head of the new colony which was to establish a Danish trade with the Greenlanders.

In May 1721, with his wife and four children, and about forty other persons, he sailed from Bergen in the *Hope*, and after a dangerous and almost disastrous voyage, they reached their distant destination. The dreams which had been awakened in many of their minds by the very name of Greenland were soon dissipated. "They found no Green-land, but endless hummocks of ice, which they coasted for weary days, and in imminent danger of shipwreck, until they landed at a small bay, and began to build on what they called "Hope's Island."

Nor was the reception which they met at the hands of the natives a whit more encouraging. As soon as they perceived that the strangers intended to remain, they used every endeavour to induce or force them to depart. Some of them feared that it was a mission of retaliation, to avenge past injuries inflicted on seamen who had touched upon their coasts. The angekoks, who were the magicians and priests of the country, tried every method of intimidation and resistance. The besotted natives listened with the most provoking apathy to the missionary's appeals, or else avoided his presence altogether. Pilfering and dishonesty of every sort were added to the general difficulties which had to be encountered. A new and difficult language had to be first conquered and then christianized; for it lacked the necessary words in which to express the simplest elements of religious truth.

For two years Hans Egede had to labour all alone, but he devoted himself to his work with heroic patience. He visited the filthy huts of the Greenlanders in order to win their confidence and acquire their language. He took native youths into his own house, and induced them to learn, by offering the tempting reward of a fish-hook for every letter that was acquired. He soon obtained sufficient knowledge of the language to enable him to translate into it several portions of the Holy Scriptures, as well as the creed and some prayers and hymns. With the help of his son he made rough sketches of Scripture scenes, and then endeavoured to explain them. He followed the people in their hunting and fishing expeditions, and tried in every way to influence them for good. But still neither the mission nor the colony made progress. The colonists became discontented, and resolved to return, and Hans Egede's own heart began at times to fail. It was at this crisis that his noble wife became his truest helper. She never lost her hope in God, or her confidence in the mission, and her prayers and her resolution were his best encouragements. Just as the last rays of hope seemed dying out, two vessels arrived from Denmark, not only bringing provisions for the colony, but bearing the welcome news that the trade would be sustained, and that the king would support the mission.

For a time things looked brighter. Some additional missionaries came to Egede's assistance, and the colony was reinforced by new immigrants. Preparations were made for erecting a fort and garrison for their protection, and externally the colony seemed to thrive. But still little or no impression was made upon the heathen. The missionaries were scoffed at and insulted by their hearers, who seemed to take a pleasure in turning them and their message into ridicule, and to possess a peculiar aptitude for rough-and-ready satire. Their angekoks, they said, had been in heaven, and had seen no Son of God, nor had they observed that the firmament was out of repair, or that the world was in any danger of ever coming to an end. Let them have but good food, and they wanted nothing else. If they required a heaven, they had one of their own in the depths of the ocean, where dwelt Torngarnsuk and his mother; where there was perpetual summer, and fishes, and reindeer, and their beloved seals, all to be caught without any toil, and even to be found in a great kettle, boiling alive!

All this was most discouraging, and yet we can see in it an element of gracious discipline. The one fault of Hans Egede's character was that, like Francis Xavier, he was at first too much inclined to lean on human help. He had resorted moreover for this very reason to threats and severities in dealing with his most provoking hearers, and even went the length of inflicting corporal punishment upon some of his more violent opponents. He was to learn that it was not by means of this kind, nor by the royal power which he threatened to invoke for their chastisement, that his rude hearers were to be won, or the gentle reign of Jesus Christ established amongst them.

Christian VI. had now ascended the throne of Denmark, and deeming that the commercial speculation of the mission was a bad one, withdrew his kingly aid, and issued a mandate that the colonists should return home. Hans Egede might remain if he chose, and provisions for one year were assigned to him, but with the distinct understanding that no further aid could or would be granted. This was another crisis, not only in his life, but in the history of the undertaking. None of the colonists were willing to remain with him, and he must now decide whether he should remain alone upon that desolate and icebound shore, or abandon the great enterprise of his life. To his eternal honour, and still more to that of his heroic wife, who sustained him in his decision, he chose the former alternative, and in doing so became the father and founder of the Greenland mission.

It was ultimately arranged that ten sailors might remain with him, but his missionary colleagues and all the colonists returned home. The king subsequently relented so far as to send a vessel in the following year, with some supplies; but unfortunately that vessel had on board a native boy who had gone to Copenhagen with the returning colonists, and who now brought back with him the dreadful scourge of the smallpox, which was a disease hitherto unknown in Greenland. It spread rapidly and fatally through the country; whole villages were depopulated; the natives in terror and despair stabbed themselves to death, or plunged into the sea to put a speedy end to their sufferings. For forty leagues north and south the devastation spread, until some thousands had perished beneath the new and fearful plague. Worst of all, the Greenlanders laid the blame of the visitation upon the helpless missionary, and all hope of gaining a hearing for the Gospel amongst them seemed to be at an end.

But out of apparent evil sprang real good. Hans Egede and the two Moravian missionaries, who had by this time come to his assistance, gave practical proof in this dreadful emergency of what Christianity really was. They tended the sick; they took them into their own homes; they waited on them and nursed them day and night, at the constant risk of their own lives. It was a new thing amongst the savages of Greenland, and stood in striking contrast to the selfishness of their own relatives and friends, who had deserted them in the hour of danger. "Thou hast done for us," they exclaimed to the missionary, "what our own people would not do; for thou hast fed us when we had nothing to eat; thou hast buried our dead, who else would have been consumed by the dogs, foxes, and ravens; thou hast also instructed us in the knowledge of God, and hast told us of a better life!"

We have spoken of the Moravians and their timely help. As the mission which Hans Egede so nobly commenced was carried to its ultimate success by means of their labour, it is only fair to take some additional notice here of their great and unprecedented work. Count Zinzendorf had given a home in Lusatia to the remnant of the persecuted followers of Huss and Jerome of Prague. Scarcely had these exiles found a resting-place, than they resolved on missionary enterprise amongst the heathen. The Count, who had cast in his lot with the exiles whom he had sheltered, was attending the coronation of Christian VI., at Copenhagen, when he saw two Greenlanders who had been baptized by Egede, and he learned with regret that the new monarch had resolved on abandoning the mission to Greenland. About the same time a negro from St. Thomas's had told the Count's domestics about the sufferings of the slaves in the West Indies, and of their earnest desire to be instructed in the Christian religion. The story of the Greenland mission was recited by the Count to the congregation of Moravians at Herrnhut, and the story of the unfortunate slaves was told to them in simple but touching language by the poor negro. Within a year the first missionary labourers were preaching both in Greenland and the West Indies, and in ten years these humble but illustrious exiles had established missions in South America, Surinam, Lapland, Tartary, Algiers, Guinea, the Cape of Good Hope, and amongst the Red Indian tribes. Their success has been commensurate with their zeal. "Numbering only about 10,000 in Europe, it is calculated that they have already sent out 2,000 agents; that one in every forty of their community is a missionary to the heathen; and that there are some 57,000 in pagan lands who have been converted by their instrumentality, or are receiving instruction at their hands." No Christian community has had a monopoly in the work of missions, but the Moravian brethren must be allowed to stand supreme in this noble and blessed work.

Cowper has immortalized them in his glorious lines:—

> . . . . " See Germany send forth
> Her sons to pour it on the farthest North ;
> Fired with a zeal peculiar, they defy
> The rage and rigor of a polar sky,
> And plant successfully sweet Sharon's rose
> On icy plains, and in eternal snows ! "

It was from this self-sacrificing body of men that Hans Egede in A.D. 1732 received his devoted assistants. Some idea of their spirit and devotedness may be formed from the answers which they gave Count Pless when he questioned them at Copenhagen concerning their projected voyage to Greenland. "How do you intend," he said, "to get a livelihood?" "By the labour of our hands, and by God's blessing," was the reply. "We mean," they added, "to build a house, and cultivate the land." "But there is no wood to build a house with," said the Count. "Then we shall dig a hole in the earth," they answered, "and lodge there." Nor was this boasting vain. Their subsequent labours and hardships, all cheerfully endured, showed how thoroughly the missionary spirit had possessed them. It is told, amongst other incidents of their life, that for want of a tent they had frequently to lay themselves down in a hole in the snow; and when that was stopped up by more driven snow, they were obliged to rise and warm themselves by running. It is further recorded of them, that they trained themselves to eat seals' flesh; and that when they prepared their scanty stock of oatmeal with train oil, it was a luxury compared to the tallow candles which they had been long obliged to use for the same purpose.

They came to Greenland in good time; for Hans Egede's health, after thirteen years of unexampled toil, was failing fast, and the great sorrow of his life was at hand. His wife, who had been the companion of his labours and the strengthener of his faith, who had so strongly opposed his first missionary ardour, and then encouraged it with a zeal and determination which far outstripped and surpassed that opposition, was taken from him, and he himself was smitten down by a painful and troublesome disease; and now he must resign his labours, and carry back her hallowed dust to his native land, and bequeath his work and hers to other hands. In 1736 he sailed for Copenhagen, after preaching on a remarkable text: "I said, I have spent my strength for nought and in vain; yet surely my judgment is with the Lord, and my work with my God" (Isa. xlix. 4). Nothing could more exactly describe the work of Egede. To the eyes of man it appeared a failure, but in the sight of God it was a success. He laboured, and some would say it was in vain, but his work was with his God, and in due time the results of it were seen. It mattered little that he himself was not permitted to witness these results. It was not for fame, nor even for success, that he had laboured, but for the honour and glory of his Lord; and he was not disappointed. Immediately after his last sermon he baptized a Greenland boy; it was the first baptism which the Moravians had witnessed in Greenland, but it was the pledge of many more which they were privileged to behold, and it was the first-fruits of a noble harvest which they were permitted to reap. The people who once regarded letters as magic soon learned to read and write. Those who scoffed at the missionary soon began to accept his message. The angekoks vanished before the advance of truth, and the cruelties of heathenism gave way to the charities of Christian life. A more unpropitious field for labour cannot possibly be imagined, and yet few more successful ones have rewarded the toil of the Christian husbandman.

Hans Egede, though he had to quit the scene of his labours, still aided the missionary enterprise. He prevailed on the king to found a missionary seminary at Copenhagen, where young men might be taught the language of the Greenlanders, and he himself became the chief instructor in it. His son was induced by his father's example and persuasions to adopt the missionary life, and to devote himself to the care of the infant Church in Greenland, of which he became eventually the bishop. The aged missionary himself retired after some years to the island of Falster, where he died at the age of seventy-three, respected and beloved, and leaving behind him a name as illustrious for faith and patience as for devotedness and zeal.

XII.

CHRISTIAN FREDERIC SCHWARTZ.
A.D. 1750—1798.

THE missionary hero whose life we are about to sketch was a link between the missions of the past and those of our own time, and therefore a review of his labours will be a suitable sequel and close to the series of papers which have been already presented. He was pre-eminently a typical man, and both his own character and that of his work have rendered him one of the most remarkable personages in the history of missions. He lacked indeed the fire and fervour of some who went before him, and could not boast of the scholarship and accomplishments of some who came after him; but he far excelled them in all the sober excellences and wise qualifications of a great and master mind. To the genius of a statesman he united the unworldliness of an apostle, and to the firmness of a ruler he added the tenderness of a spiritual father. Whilst he lived he was loved and honoured, and when he died he was almost worshipped by those who had come under the charm of his life.

Christian Frederic Schwartz was a man of whom any church or country might be proud; but in reality he can be claimed by several. He was by birth a German, by ordination a Danish clergyman, and by long connection with " The Christian Knowledge Society" a labourer for the Church of England. This triple connection consorted well with the many-sidedness of his character, and furnished, as we shall see, abundant opportunities and aids to his far-reaching usefulness.

Providence was evidently preparing him from an early age for the grand future that lay before him, and the influences were manifold and strong which had already shaped his course before he himself was aware of it. On her dying bed, his pious mother dedicated him to God, and solemnly charged her husband and her pastor to bring him up under the remembrance of that dedication, and to train him for the Christian ministry, if he showed any aptitude and desire for it. His father inured him from his earliest years to those habits of self-denial and simplicity which were afterwards of such value to him in his devoted and life-long labours. Brought alternately under the awakening and the chilling influences of different teachers, his mind passed through various phases of religious experience; but he was preserved from open sin, and cultivated, though in a spasmodic way, the better impressions of his earlier years.

He had been removed, in 1742, when sixteen years of age, from his native town of Sonnenburg, where he had acquired some knowledge of Hebrew, Greek, and Latin, to a higher school at Custrin, in order to prepare for the University, and it was here that he was brought under the influences which more directly governed his future life. One of the syndics of Custrin had been educated at Halle, and Schwartz was brought into familiar intercourse with his daugher. There was no romance or sentiment in their friendship; but she lovingly set herself to influence the young student for good, and by God's blessing persuaded him to surrender himself fully to the service of his Redeemer. Amongst the books which she put in his hand was the history of the famous Orphan House, founded by Francke at Halle, and the perusal of it inspired him with the desire of completing his studies in that place. Accordingly, in 1746, he went to Halle, where the next two or three years of his life were happily and diligently spent, and where he met the indefatigable missionary Schultze, who had spent twenty years in India, and was then engaged in bringing out an edition of the Tamil Bible. Schultze soon perceived the early promise of the young student's character, and persuaded him to learn Tamil and aid him in his work. It was under these influences and during this occupation that his mind was drawn to the missionary enterprise. The Danish College of Missions had requested Francke to select suitable men for their mission at Tranquebar, and both he and Schultze concurred in the belief that young Schwartz was eminently fitted for such work. When they proposed it to him, he resolved to seek his father's consent, and if he obtained it to go out to India.

Returning to Sonnenburg, he laid the matter before his father. Christian was his eldest son, and regarded as the future stay of the family; every earthly consideration seemed to tell against his son's proposal, but he determined to give it a prayerful consideration. Three days were spent by him in his solitary chamber, where, no doubt, amidst his parental yearnings, the memories of his wife's last wishes recurred with full force to his mind; and when at length he came forth to announce his decision, he laid his hand upon the head of the boy who had been his joy and pride, gave him his parting blessing, and charged him to forget "his own country and his father's house," and to go forth in the name of the Lord to win many souls to Christ.

Young Schwartz, with that self-abnegation which was to be his pre-eminent characteristic, resigned his share in his patrimony to his brothers and sisters, refused tempting offers which were now made to him in the ministry at home, was ordained with two others by the Danish bishop at Copenhagen on the 17th of September, 1749, and after bidding a long and last adieu to all his friends, sailed for India in the following November. He visited England on his way, and was detained for some months, during which he made the acquaintance of the King's German chaplain, Mr. Zeigenhagen, and was introduced to the Society for Promoting Christian Knowledge, with which in after days he was to be so intimately associated.

Schwartz and his companions improved their opportunities on ship-board for their own good and that of their fellow-voyagers, and arrived at Tranquebar on the 8th of October, 1750. The state of things in

India was dark enough; the trading companies who had established themselves at various points were only careful about their business, and did not regard the spiritual welfare of the natives. There were twenty English regiments in Hindoostan, but not a single chaplain. We need scarcely add that the idea of an episcopate for India had not been even conceived; the lives of the Europeans were vile to a degree that can scarcely now be understood, and formed the most formidable barrier to the spread of Christianity amongst the natives. Two things, however, were favourable. The policy which took its rise in the renewal of the East India Company's charter of 1793, and which eventually caused Schwartz much trouble, had not been initiated, and there was as yet no complicity on the part of the British Government with the idolatrous practices of the heathen. Moreover the Danish authorities lent their countenance and aid to missionary endeavours, and frequent letters passed between the royal family at Copenhagen and the faithful men who were proclaiming the Gospel in India.

Schwartz set himself with determined energy to conquer the language, and to make himself master of the intricate mythology of the natives. Such was his success in the former pursuit, that within four months after his arrival he preached in Tamil, and was soon able to catechize the children in the same tongue. Indeed, full justice has never been done to the marvellous linguistic acquirements of our missionary. He conquered English (which he spoke and wrote like an Englishman) in order to preach and minister to our troops. He made himself master of Persian, and that gave him a ready introduction to the courts of Mahommedan princes. He had such command of Hindoostanee, that for this as well as other reasons he was selected by the British Government for most difficult embassies. He early learned the Indo-Portuguese, in order to be useful to the mixed race who were descended from Portuguese and Hindoos. Many of these were

Romanists, and to them Schwartz pointed out "how widely the Romish Church has deviated from the pure doctrine of the Gospel."

It was a characteristic of Schwartz, that whatever he did he did it *thoroughly*. Even his sermons for the natives were most carefully prepared. His hours from morning to night were appropriated to different duties, and he had the peculiar faculty of making others work as well as himself. Whilst at Tranquebar, it was his custom to go on foot, with one or more companions, through the native villages, preaching and conversing with the people, and reasoning with priests and worshippers, even in their own pagodas. He had considerable success; village after village embraced the truth; idols were deserted, and hymns of praise to the true God replaced the profane and licentious songs of the heathen temples. But Schwartz saw that the real difficulty was in men's hearts. "If," says he, "idolatry were only an error of the *understanding*, the greater number of the heathen would already have renounced it. It is because it is a work of the flesh that they hold to it." He was eminently useful in quickening other missions into new life, and his visit to Ceylon was accompanied by most valuable results.

He had been labouring for sixteen years in India, however, before his most important work began. It was in 1766 that he came into connection with the Christian Knowledge Society, and from that day forward his sphere of labour lay chiefly in Trichinopoly and Tanjore. He was now forty years of age, and though simple in his habits, was no ascetic, and his conversation upon secular as well as on sacred subjects was confessedly charming. We have the advantage of possessing a most graphic description of his person, and from an eyewitness: "His garb, which was pretty well worn, seemed foreign and old-fashioned, but in every other respect his appearance was the reverse of all that could be called forbidding or morose. Figure to yourself a stout, well-made man, somewhat above the middle height, erect in carriage and address, with a complexion rather dark, though healthy, black curled hair, and a manly, engaging countenance expressive of unaffected candour, ingenuousness, and benevolence, and you will have an idea of what Mr. Schwartz appeared to be at first sight. At Trichinopoly he had much to do with narrow means. His whole income was *ten pagodas per month*, or about £48 a year. He obtained of the commanding officer, who perhaps was ordered to furnish him with quarters, a room in an old Gentoo building which was just large enough to hold his bed and himself, and in which few men could stand upright. With this apartment he was contented. A dish of rice and vegetables dressed after the manner of the natives was what he could always cheerfully sit down to, and a piece of dimity, dyed black, and other materials of the same homely sort, sufficed him for an annual supply of clothing. Thus easily provided as to temporalities, his only care was to do the work of an evangelist."

Schwartz' work was quiet—indeed, almost plodding; but it was earnest, persevering, and prayerful. To a shrewd judgment he added a loving charity, and a ready tact that accommodated itself, but without compromise of principle, to every variety of circumstance. He could faithfully reprove kings and princes for their vices, and yet win and retain their esteem. He could fearlessly expose the follies of Hinduism and Mahommedanism, and yet obtain a respectful hearing for the message of salvation. He could and did devote himself to the reclamation of professing Christians, aud still keep steadily in view the grand object of his life in the evangelization of the heathen. And so converts were made, and congregations were gathered, and churches erected, and schools established, ann orphanages founded, until the wilderness around him began to "blossom as the rose."

He had too much sagacity to be imposed on by pretenders, and yet too much love for souls to repel any inquirers concerning whom there was the slightest ground of hope. To use his own expression, he met such cases with a "kind severity." His influence over his own flocks was unbounded. He was their patriarch as well as their pastor. "Will you go to the royal court, or be punished by me?" was the alternative proposed to offenders. "O padre, you punish me!" was the invariable reply. "Give him twenty strokes," said the padre, and it was done. And yet this was the man who could listen like a father, and sympathise like a brother, wherever there was human sorrow or deep anxiety of soul. Firm, humorous, sympathizing, he had smiles for the happy and tears for the sad.

It has been well said that "his known probity and truthfulness won him the confidence of three most dissimilar parties—a suspicious tyrant, an oppressed people, and the military and diplomatic directors of the British Empire in the East."

"Do not send to me," said Hyder Ali, "any of your agents, for I do not trust their words or treaties; but if you wish me to listen to your proposals, send to me the missionary of whose character I have heard so much from every one: him I will trust and receive. Send me the *Christian!*" Amidst the wars of the Carnatic he was allowed to pass from camp to camp without molestation; the vindictive Nabob himself issuing this order, "Permit the venerable Father Schwartz to pass unhindered, and show him respect and kindness; for he is a holy man, and means no harm to my government."

When famine was mowing down its thousands in Tanjore, and the people refused to bring in provisions to the rapacious officers who had so often plundered and deceived them, the rajah exclaimed, "We all, you and I, have lost our credit; let us try whether the inhabitants will trust Mr. Schwartz." He sent a *carte blanche* to the missionary, empowering him to make any arrangements he thought proper. Within two days a thousand oxen were placed at his disposal, and eighty thousand measures of rice brought in to the starving garrison.

When the Collaries, a caste of thieves, had revolted against the oppression of Tuljajee's government, the influence of Schwartz brought back seven thousand of them to their allegiance in a single day, and when he exhorted them to industry and labour, they replied, "You have shown us kindness, and you will never have reason to repent it. We will work night and day to show our regard for you;" and they kept their word.

Amongst our soldiers his influence was unbounded. To use the language of his biographer, "he could persuade whole garrisons." The officers of the 48th Regiment declared that corporal punishment had ceased amongst their men from the time that they came under his religious instruction. Again and again he was employed by the authorities upon the most difficult and delicate embassies to native princes, and these he undertook from no motive of personal advantage or ambition, but, as he himself declared, " to preserve the blessings of peace," and "to announce the gospel of God my Saviour in many parts where it had not been known before." And so it came to pass that, as before, amidst the hovels around Trichinopoly, so now amidst the marble halls of Seringapatam and the gorgeous palaces of Tanjore this more than statesman served his country, and proclaimed to kings and princes the story of redeeming love. " Happy indeed would it be for India," wrote the British resident at Tanjore, "happy for the Company, and for the Rajah himself, if Schwartz possessed the whole authority, and were invested with power to execute all the measures which his wisdom and benevolence would suggest."

As to his disinterestedness, it was beyond suspicion, and he took care to make it so. An officer, to whom he had been spiritually useful, left him a legacy; Schwartz declined it. A native minister of state tendered him a valuable present; he accepted a nosegay in its place. Hyder Ali sent him three hundred rupees to defray the expenses of his mission to his court; the missionary, finding that it would be a breach of etiquette to send it back, handed it over to his own government. He had ministered to the sick and dying during the siege of Madura, and a sum of two hundred and forty pounds was allotted to him as his well-deserved portion of the Nabob's gift to the British troops; he appropriated the gift to the support of his schools and orphanage. When the Madras authorities, without any solicitation, awarded him a hundred pounds a year as chaplain to the forces, he devoted one half of it to the use of his native congregations; and whenever he went on a political mission for the Government, he systematically refused to accept a farthing beyond his travelling expenses. "Let the cause of Christ be my heir," was one of his last utterances upon his dying bed.

Bishop Heber, who went out to India rather prejudiced against the character of Schwartz, as if he had been too much of a political agent, has left the following remarkable testimony as the result of a most careful investigation:—" He was one of the most active and fearless, as he was one of the most successful, missionaries who have appeared since the days of the Apostles. To say that he was disinterested in regard of money is nothing; he was perfectly careless of power, and renown never seemed to affect him, even so far as to induce an outward show of humility. His temper was perfectly simple, open, and cheerful, and in his political negotiations (employments which he never sought, but which fell in his way) he never pretended to impartiality; but acted as the avowed, though certainly the successful and judicious, agent of the orphan prince committed to his care."

This mention of the orphan prince, Sarfojee, reminds us of the wondrous influence which Schwartz exercised over Tuljajee, the Rajah of Tanjore, who used to call him his "own padre." On his deathbed the rajah committed his adopted child to the missionary's care, saying, "This is not my son, but yours; into your hands I deliver him." It is well known how faithfully, fearlessly, and lovingly he fulfilled that trust, standing for years, not only between the boy and his heathen oppressors, but between him and the unjust decision of the British authorities. Schwartz did not live to see it, but his energy and his remonstrances were the means of restoring Sarfojee to his rightful throne. His letters to the young prince are models of wisdom, tenderness, and statesmanship; and though, like his predecessors, Sarfojee was only "almost persuaded" to be a Christian, he never ceased to revere his teacher's character, and to further, long after his decease, all the objects which he had at heart. On the stone which covers the ashes of the venerable missionary are written the following lines by his admiring pupil—the first ever written in English by a Hindoo prince :—

> "Firm wast thou, humble and wise,
> Honest, pure, free from disguise;
> Father of orphans, the widow's support,
> Comfort in sorrow of every sort :

> To the benighted, dispenser of light,
> Doing and pointing to that which is right.
> Blessing to princes, to people, to me,
> May I, my father, be worthy of thee,
> Wisheth and prayeth thy Sarabojee."

The prince caused a splendid monument, by Flaxman, to be erected to the memory of his benefactor. It represents the death-bed scene in which the young prince and the administration of his kingdom were committed to Schwartz. The East India Company placed another, by Bacon, to the honour of this missionary hero, "whose life," as the inscription truly records, "was one continued effort to imitate the example of his blessed Master." He died in the seventy-second year of his age, after fifty years of unceasing labour, with the sacred, songs of his fatherland upon his lips, and the peace of God abiding in his heart. The heathens paid divine honours to his memory and made offerings at his shrine. Between six and seven thousand converts rewarded his labours, not to speak of those whom his companions won over to the truth. His memory is still revered by Christians, Hindoos, and Mahommedans. He laid broad and deep the foundations of the Christian Church in India; was the first to organize the commencement of a native ministry for Hindustan, and left it as his dying testimony, that the work of the missionary is "THE MOST HONOURABLE AND BLESSED SERVICE IN WHICH ANY HUMAN BEING CAN BE EMPLOYED IN THIS WORLD."

THE END.

Now ready, Third Edition, *in crown 8vo, paper* 1s., *cloth* 1s. 6d.

ANCIENT MONUMENTS AND THEIR TESTIMONY TO HOLY WRIT.

WITH ILLUSTRATIONS.

BY THE RIGHT REV. W. PAKENHAM WALSH, D.D.,
Bishop of Ossory, Ferns, and Leighlin.

"The ample information contained in the book is imparted simply and in readable style, but can at the same time lay claim to scientific accuracy. We heartily commend it to general attention."—*Evening Mail.*

"One of the most remarkable, if not THE most remarkable, confirmations of Bible truths which has appeared in our time."—*Irish Church Advocate.*

"We heartily thank the Dean; and when our friends have read his book, they will heartily thank us for recommending it."—*Church of England Sunday School Magazine.*

"We cannot speak too highly of the little book which lies before us. Written with scholarly accuracy."—*Daily Express.*

"It is a work of great importance—eminently useful, and deeply interesting to all who study Holy Scripture.'—*Cork Constitution.*

Eleventh Edition, with Illustrations and Maps, 1s., *cloth limp* 1s. 6d.

THE MOABITE STONE,
Erected by Mesha, King of Moab, 960 B.C., Discovered at Dibon, A.D. 1868.

TWO LECTURES

BY THE RIGHT REV. W. PAKENHAM WALSH, D.D.,
Bishop of Ossory, Ferns, and Leighlin.

"Many will thank Mr. Walsh for gathering into these pages a very valuable and instructive essay on this, the latest and most valuable archæological discovery of the day in connection with the historical verity of the Old Testament Scripture."—*Irish Ecclesiastical Gazette.*

DUBLIN: GEORGE HERBERT, 117, GRAFTON STREET.
LONDON: HAMILTON, ADAMS, & CO.; AND J. NISBET & CO.

THE ENGLISHMAN'S CRITICAL AND EXPOSITORY BIBLE CYCLOPÆDIA. Compiled and Written by the Rev. A. R. FAUSSET, M.A. With Six Hundred Illustrative Woodcuts. 4vo, cloth, price 18s.

ZECHARIAH AND HIS PROPHECIES. Especially the Messianic, considered in relation to Modern Criticism. With a critically-revised Translation of the original Hebrew, and a Critical and Grammatical Commentary on the entire book. THE BAMPTON LECTURES for 1878. By the Rev. C. H. H. WRIGHT, B.D., M.A., Ph.D. Demy 8vo, cloth, price 14s.

THE DOCTRINE OF RETRIBUTION; Philosophically Considered. THE BAMPTON LECTURES for 1875. By the Rev. W. JACKSON, M.A., F.R.S. Second Edition. 8vo, cloth, price 10s. 6d.

THE PHILOSOPHY OF NATURAL THEOLOGY. An Essay in Confutation of the Scepticism of the Present Day. By the same AUTHOR. 8vo, cloth, price 12s.

MACDONALD'S LIFE AND WRITINGS OF ST. JOHN. Edited with an Introduction, by the Very Rev. Dean HOWSON, D.D. With Five Maps and Thirty fullpage Illustrations. Royal 8vo, cloth, price 21s.

SACRED STREAMS: The Ancient and Modern History of the Rivers of the Bible. By PHILIP HENRY GOSSE, F.R.S. With Forty-four Illustrations, and a Map. Crown 8vo, cloth, price 7s. 6d.; gilt edges, price 8s.

GODET'S STUDIES ON THE NEW TESTAMENT. Edited by the Hon. and Rev. Canon LYTTELTON, M.A. Second Thousand. Crown 8vo, cloth, price 7s. 6d.

LONDON:
HODDER AND STOUGHTON, 27, PATERNOSTER ROW.

HEROES OF THE MISSION FIELD. By The Right Rev. W. PAKENHAM WALSH, D.D., Bishop of Ossory. Crown 8vo, cloth, price 5s.

A MEMOIR OF ACHILLES DAUNT, D.D., Late Dean of Cork. With Selections from his Sermons and Letters. Edited by the Rev. F. R. Wynne, M.A. Crown 8vo, cloth.

LETTERS TO A YOUNG CLERGYMAN. By the Rev. CANON MILLER, D.D. Crown 8vo, cloth, price 5s.

CHRISTIAN SUNSETS; or, The Last Hours of Believers. By the Rev. JAMES FLEMING, D.D. Crown 8vo, cloth, price 5s.

A POPULAR EXPOSITION OF THE EPISTLE TO THE SEVEN CHURCHES OF ASIA. By the Rev. Prof. PLUMPTRE, D.D. Crown 8vo, cloth, price 5s.

SIDE-LIGHTS ON SCRIPTURE TEXTS. By FRANCIS JACOX, B.A. Crown 8vo, cloth, price 7s. 6d.

THE PROPHETS OF CHRISTENDOM. Sketches of Eminent Preachers. By the Rev. W. BOYD CARPENTER, M.A., Vicar of St. James's, Holloway. Crown 8vo, cloth, price 5s.

THE CHRISTIAN CREED: Its Theory and Practice. With a Preface on some Present Dangers of the English Church. By the Rev. Professor STANLEY LEATHES, M.A., D.D. Crown 8vo, cloth, price 7s. 6d.

LONDON:
HODDER AND STOUGHTON, 27, PATERNOSTER ROW.

www.ingramcontent.com/pod-product-compliance
Lightning Source LLC
Chambersburg PA
CBHW031349230426
43670CB00006B/478